Korean
Recipes

Korean Recipes

Written by	Yun Ji-yu
Translated by	Jamie Lypka
First Published	February 2022
2nd Printed	January 2024
Publisher	Chung Kyudo
Editors	Lee Suk-hee, Kim Sook-hee, Park Inkyung
Designer	Kim Na-kyoung, Yoon Hyun-ju
Voice Actors	Kim Rae-whan, Shin So-yun, Toosix Media

DARAKWON Published by Darakwon Inc.

Darakwon Bldg., 211 Munbal-ro, Paju-si,
Gyeonggi-do, 10881 Republic of Korea
Tel: 82-2-736-2031
(Marketing Dept. ext.: 250~252 Editorial Dept. ext.: 420~426)
Fax: 82-2-732-2037

ISBN: 978-89-277-3286-0 14710
     978-89-277-3285-3 (set)

http://www.darakwon.co.kr
http://koreanbooks.darakwon.co.kr
﹡ Visit the Darakwon homepage to learn about our other publications and
promotions and to download the contents of MP3 format.

Yun Ji-yu

Korean Recipes

DARAKWON

PREFACE

전 세계적으로 드라마와 가요에서 시작된 한류의 열풍은 음식, 언어, 문화 산업 등 다양한 분야로 확산되고 있습니다. 특히 집에서 여가를 보내며 직접 요리를 하려는 사람들이 많아지면서 한국 음식을 만들어 보고, 맛보고 싶어 하는 외국인들 역시 점점 늘어나고 있습니다.

⟨Easy & Fun Korean Recipes⟩는 이러한 경향을 반영하여 한국 음식을 직접 만들어 보면서 한국어를 배울 수 있도록 구성한 책입니다. 앞서 필자가 집필한 ⟨Easy & Fun Korean Penmanship⟩이 전세계 초급 한국어 학습자들로부터 많은 인기를 얻은 것에 감사하며, 초급 한국어 학습자들이 좀 더 재미있게 한국어를 공부할 수 있는 방법을 고민하다가 이 책을 집필하게 되었습니다.

⟨Easy & Fun Korean Recipes⟩는 외국인들의 선호도가 높은 한국 음식을 중심으로 총 40개의 요리 목록을 선정하고 이를 재료별로 나누어 제시했습니다. 그리고 각 요리마다 필요한 재료와 만드는 방법을 상세히 소개하여 관련 어휘를 익히고 한국어 표현을 연습해 볼 수 있도록 했습니다. 또한 한식의 조리법이 낯설거나 자세한 과정을 확인하고 싶은 학습자들을 위해 조리 과정을 동영상으로 제공하였습니다. 교재 구성에 맞춘 조리 과정을 차근차근 따라가다 보면 어느새 한국 요리와 한국어에 익숙해질 수 있을 것입니다.

한국어 교육자로서 요리가 중심이 된 책을 쓴다는 것이 쉬운 일은 아니었습니다. 원고를 쓰고, 그에 맞춰 직접 요리하는 과정을 동영상과 사진으로 촬영하는 것은 많은 시간과 노력을 필요로 하는 일이었습니다. 그만큼 이 책을 통해 한국 음식과 한국어에 관심을 가지고 계신 많은 분들이 '한식'을 직접 만들어 보고 그 맛을 경험할 수 있는 좋은 계기가 될 수 있기를 바랍니다.

이 책이 완성되기까지 용기를 주시고 응원해 주신 부모님께 감사드립니다. 특히 어릴 때부터 재료 다듬는 법부터 요리의 과정을 틈틈이 일러 주셨던 어머니의 가르침에 감사드립니다. 또한 이 책이 출간될 수 있도록 끝까지 함께 해 주신 다락원 한국어 출판부 편집진께도 감사의 마음을 전합니다.

윤지유

The Korean Wave, which began to spread worldwide through TV dramas and music, is expanding into various fields, including food, language, and cultural industries. In particular, as more and more people are spending their leisure time at home and cooking for themselves, the number of foreigners hoping to try making and tasting Korean food is of course continuing to increase.

Reflecting this trend, *Easy & Fun Korean Recipes* is a book designed to allow readers to learn Korean while trying to cook Korean food for themselves. I am grateful for the popularity that my previous book, *Easy & Fun Korean Penmanship*, received from beginner-level Korean-language learners from around the world, and I came to write this book after considering ways to make Korean language study a bit more entertaining for these beginner-level learners.

Easy & Fun Korean Recipes is centered around a selected list of a total of 40 Korean dishes that are highly favored by foreigners, presented to the reader as divided by ingredients. It was also made so that for each dish, the required ingredients and method of preparation are introduced in detail, so that readers can learn related vocabulary and practice Korean expressions. And for readers who are unfamiliar with Korean cooking methods or want to verify the steps in greater detail, videos of the cooking process are provided. If you follow along step by step with the recipes matched to the textbook's composition, you'll soon find yourself becoming familiar with Korean cooking and language.

As a Korean-language educator, writing a book about cooking was no easy task. Writing the manuscript and personally filming and photographing the cooking process took a lot of time and effort. As such, I hope that this book will present a good opportunity for many people with an interest in Korean food and language to prepare and experience the taste of Korean food for themselves.

I thank my parents for encouraging me and cheering me on through this book's completion. I am particularly thankful for my mother's instructions, here and there from the time I was young, in the preparation of ingredients and the cooking process. I also express my thanks to the editors on Darakwon's Korean Editorial Team for sticking with me until the end so that this book could be published.

Yun Ji-yu

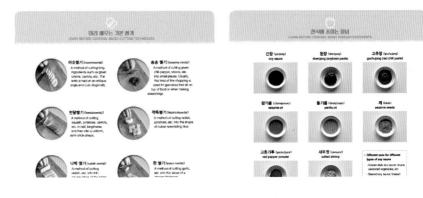

음식 소개 ◆ Introduction of Food

각 요리의 첫 페이지는 완성 음식 사진과 함께 해당 요리
에 대한 간략한 설명을 제시하여 요리에 대한 이해를 높
였습니다. 총 40가지의 요리는 고유 명사 명칭으로 표기
됩니다.

The first page for each dish provides a picture of the
completed dish and a brief description to enhance
understanding. The name of each of the 40 dishes
is displayed in proper noun format.

저자가 직접 진행한 해당 요리 영상은 QR 코드를
통해 확인할 수 있습니다.

A video of the author personally preparing
the dish can be accessed via QR code.

· BIBIMBAP ·

Bibimbap is a food that is made by placing different seasoned vegetable
meat on top of rice, adding gochujang or soy sauce, and mixing before

In the past, it was called "goldongban" instead of "bibimbap," mean
"to mix dizzily." Bibimbap is a representative Korean food, and is popul
Korean people and of course with foreigners as well. If making the sea
vegetables is difficult, it can also be mixed and eaten with variou
stir-fried vegetables and gochujang instead.

한식 요리의 기본 ◆ Korean Cooking Basics

총 40가지의 요리가 수록되어 있습니다. 각 요리를 배우기 전에 알아두어야 할 한식 요리의 기본인 '썰기, 조리 용어, 계량, 양념' 등에 대한 내용과 한식 상차림의 기본인 '김치' 와 '밥 짓기'의 내용을 담았습니다.

Contains a total of 40 different dishes. Includes information on cutting techniques, cooking terms, measurements, seasoning, and other must-know basics before learning each dish, as well as information on kimchi and making rice, the basics of a Korean table setting.

EDIENTS

(2)
00g) 2 bowls
f steamed rice
g 150 grams of beef
/3 carrot
t 1/3 Korean squash
hrooms
/2 onion
same oil
gs
inch of salt
ooking oil

Marinade

EEF MARINADE
espoon soy sauce
tablespoon sugar
은
ushed garlic
sesame oil
d black pepper

EASONED SPINACH
grams of spinach
espoons soy sauce
me oil
ch of ground

BIM GOCHUJANG
hujang
ablespoon sugar
ame oil

H SOY SAUCE
spoons soy sauce
ablespoon sugar
me oil

준비 PREPARATION

◆ 소고기는 가늘게 썰거나 다진 고기를 이용한다.
Cut beef into thin slices or use ground beef.

◆ 당근, 양파, 표고버섯은 채를 썰고, 호박은 반달썰기 한다. 시금치는 다듬어 씻는다.
Slice the carrots, onions, and shiitake mushrooms, and cut the Korean squash into half-circle slices. Trim and clean the spinach.

◆ 채소 재료는 다른 채소로 대신하거나 빼도 된다.
Vegetables can be substituted with others or omitted.

요리 COOKING

1 소고기에 고기 양념을 모두 넣고 무쳐서 재워 둔다.
   Add all the marinade to the beef, season it, and leave it to rest.

2 시금치는 끓는 물에 1~2분 정도 데쳐서 찬물에 헹궈 물기를 꼭 짠다. 그 다음 간장,
   참기름, 깨소금을 넣고 무친다.
   Blanch the spinach in boiling water for 1-2 minutes, rinse with cold water, and squeeze well.
   Then season with soy sauce, sesame oil, and ground sesame.

3 당근, 양파, 표고버섯과 호박은 각각 팬에 기름을 두르고 소금을 뿌려 살짝 볶는다.
   Coat the pan in oil, then lightly stir-fry the carrots, onions, shiitake mushrooms, and Korean
   squash separately, sprinkled with salt.

4 재워 둔 소고기는 프라이팬에 볶는다.
   Stir-fry the marinated beef in a frying pan.

5 비빔 고추장 또는 비빔 간장 재료를 모두 섞어 양념장을 만들고, 달걀프라이를 만든다.
   Mix all the bibim gochujang or bibim soy sauce ingredients to make a sauce, and fry an egg.

6 그릇에 밥을 담고 채소들과 소고기를 담고 달걀프라이를 올린다. 그 위에 참
   기름을 넣고 비빔 고추장 또는 비빔 간장을 곁들여 비빈다.
   Fill a bowl with steamed rice, add the stir-fried vegetables and beef, and place the fried egg on
   top. Top with sesame oil, and then garnish with bibim gochujang or bibim soy sauce and mix.

57

재료 소개 ◆ Introduction of Ingredients

각 요리의 재료를 한·영 병기로 표기하고, 양념장 등은 따로 하단에 분리하여 제시하였습니다.

The ingredients for each dish are written in Korean and English, and marinades, etc. are provided separately at the bottom.

재료별 요리 구분 ◆ Categorized by Ingredients

총 6가지의 재료 구분은 오른쪽 상단에 숫자와 색상으로 인덱스처럼 구분할 수 있게 했습니다.

A total of 6 categories of ingredients are divided in an index format, with a number and color at the top right corner of the page.

요리 과정 ◆ Cooking Process

요리는 준비 과정에 이어서 요리 본 과정을 각 단계별로 사진 자료와 함께 제시하여 보고 따라할 수 있도록 했습니다.

Following the preparation process, the cooking process is provided with photos at each stage, so that you can watch and follow along.

어휘 ◆ Vocabulary

해당 요리에서 배울 수 있는 재료와 요리 표현 어휘를 제시하였습니다. 각 재료에 대한 사진 자료와 간단한 설명으로 이해를 높였으며, 요리 표현에서는 예문을 함께 넣었습니다.

With each dish, vocabulary is provided for ingredients and cooking expressions. Each ingredient features a picture and a simple description to enhance understanding, and example sentences are included for cooking expressions.

QR 코드로 각 재료명과 표현, 예문의 음성 녹음도 바로 확인할 수 있습니다.

You can use the QR codes to check an audio recording of each ingredient name, cooking expression, and example sentence.

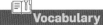

재료 INGREDIENTS

시금치 [sigeumchi]
spinach

note
Spinach, which contains many different vitamins, is eaten seasoned or boiled into soup, and is also used as a minor ingredient in japchae, gimbap, bibimbap, etc.

참기름 [chamgireum]
sesame oil

note
Sesame seeds are roasted and pressed the savory aroma strong, so this is used various foods.

요리 COOKING

Base Form	Meaning	Examples
비비다 [bibida]	to mix	• 비빔밥은 밥에 채소를 넣고 **비비세** For bibimbap, mix vegetables into rice. • 국수에 간장을 넣고 **비비면** 맛있어 If you add soy sauce to noodles and mix, good.
무치다 [muchida]	to season	• 소고기를 양념에 **무쳐서** 재워 두세 Season the beef with the marinade and le • 시금치를 간장과 참기름으로 **무쳐세** Season the spinach with soy sauce and s
만들다 [mandeulda]	to make	• 양념장을 **만드세요**. Make the marinade. • 비빔 고추장을 **만들어서** 곁들이세 Make the bibim gochujang and use as a

58

부록 ◆ Appendix

본문 요리에서 영어 번역만 들어간 각 요리 소개와 'Let's Speak Korean!'의 한국어 문법 설명에 대한 한국어 원문을 정리하였으며, 각 요리의 'Vocabulary' 색인을 제시하였습니다.

To supplement the English translations provided in the main text of the book, we've organized the Korean versions of the introductions to each dish, as well as the original Korean text from "Let's Speak Korean!" explaining the Korean grammar, and have also presented an index of the "Vocabulary" from each dish.

Let's Speak Korean!

끔 먹어요.

빔밥을 자주 먹어요? Do you eat bibimbap often?

요, 가끔 먹어요. No, I eat it occasionally.

en) and 가끔 (occasionally) are adverbs that indicate the degree to which an
r task is repeated. The following words can be used depending on the degree
ency.

안~	거의 안~	가끔	자주	100 항상 / 언제나
at all	almost never	occasionally	often	always/any time

이거 자주 해요? Do you do this often?

네, 자주 해요. / 아니요, 가끔 해요. Yes, I often do it. / No, I do it occasionally.

항상 / 언제나	전혀 안 / 거의 안

빔밥을 먹어 봤어요?

밥을 먹어 봤어요? Have you tried eating bibimbap?

비행기에서 먹어 봤어요. Yes, I tried it on a plane.

다 is an expression used to explain that something has been tried or
ced before.

em with ㅏ/ㅗ + -아 봤어요: 맑(다) + -아 봤어요 → 말아 봤어요

em with other vowels + -어 봤어요: 만들(다) + -어 봤어요 → 만들어 봤어요

- 해 봤어요: 요리하(다) → 요리해 봤어요

거제 뭐 했어요? What did you do yesterday?

김밥을 만들어 봤어요. I tried making gimbap.

미역국을 끓이다	해물파전을 부치다

Be careful!
VOWELS
ㅏ + ㅓ → ㅓ
끓이어 → 끓여
부치이어 → 부쳐

한국어로 말하기 ◆ Let's Speak Korean!

요리를 따라하며 자주 접할 수 있는 주요 한국어 표현을 쉽게 익힐 수 있도록 문법 설명과 예문을 제시하였습니다.

Grammar explanations and example sentences are provided so that you can easily master key Korean expressions that you come across frequently as you following along in your cooking.

Track 035

각 예문과 연습 대화 및 문장은 QR 코드를 통해 음성 녹음을 바로 확인할 수 있습니다.

You can check an audio recording of each example, practice dialogue, and sentence via QR code.

Track 036

59

CONTENTS

Korean Recipes

KOREAN COOKING BASICS

미리 배우는 기본 썰기
LEARN BEFORE COOKING: BASIC CUTTING TECHNIQUES

어슷썰기 [eoseutsseolgi]
A method of cutting long ingredients such as green onions, carrots, etc. The knife is held at an oblique angle and cuts diagonally.

송송 썰기 [songsong sseolgi]
A method of cutting green chili pepper, onions, etc. into small pieces. Usually, this kind of fine chopping is used for garnishes that sit on top of food or when making seasonings.

반달썰기 [bandalsseolgi]
A method of cutting squash, potatoes, carrots, etc. in half, lengthwise, and then into a uniform, semi-circle shape.

깍둑썰기 [kkakttuksseolgi]
A method of cutting radish, potatoes, etc. into the shape of cubes resembling dice.

나박 썰기 [nabak sseolgi]
A method of cutting radish, etc. into thin, square slices of the same height and length.

편 썰기 [pyeon sseolgi]
A method of cutting garlic, etc. into thin slices of a chosen thickness.

채썰기 [chaesseolgi]
A method of thinly slicing ingredients to a desired length, then stacking them up and cutting them into slender slices of a uniform thickness.

다지기 [dajigi]
A method of evenly gathering up julienned ingredients and cutting them again into a smaller size.

미리 알아 두면 유용한 요리 용어
USEFUL INFORMATION BEFORE COOKING: COOKING TERMS

한소끔 끓이다
[hansokkeum kkeurida]
A word that indicates boiling once, when boiling soups, stews, etc., used frequently when cooking soups.

한 꼬집
[han kkojip]
Means the amount of salt, sugar, etc. that you pick up by pinching your thumb and index finger together. Used when a very small amount of something is needed.

밑간
[mitkkgan]
Refers to infusing ingredients with seasoning before cooking, by marinating them in soy sauce or leaving them to rest in salt, etc. beforehand.

자작하다
[jajakada]
Means that a soup is boiled down to the degree that the ingredients just barely become visible.

무르다
[mureuda]
Means that something hard become softened.

익다
[iktta]
Refers to applying heat to raw food such as meat, vegetables, grains, etc. to change its properties and taste.

재우다
[jaeuda]
Means applying seasoning or marinade to food beforehand and leaving it for a set period of time in order to infuse it with taste.

달구다
[dalguda]
Refers to putting a frying pan over a burner and heating it up.

지지다
[jijida]
Refers to putting ingredients in a heated pan coated with oil, and cooking them by frying.

두르다
[dureuda]
Refers to adding oil to or spreading oil evenly over a frying pan.

데치다
[dechida]
Means to put vegetables, seafood, etc. into boiling water to cook them just slightly.

삶다
[samtta]
Refers to putting ingredients in water and then boiling.

치대다
[chidaeda]
Refers to massaging dough, etc. frequently until it's free of lumps and becomes viscous.

버무리다
[beomurida]
Means to mix several different ingredients together.

찌다
[jjida]
Means to cook or heat vegetables, tteok (rice cake), etc. in hot steam.

뜸 들이다
[tteum deurida]
Means to not lift the lid for some time after applying heat when boiling food or making rice, so that the contents become well cooked.

◆ 계량 Measurements

큰술 [keunsul] / 작은술 [jageunsul] tablespoon / teaspoon

1큰술 = 15ml

1/2큰술 =7ml

1작은술 = 5ml

컵 [keop] cup   1컵 = 200ml

✦ **For powders or grains**
Fill completely, then make the surface flat (level off the top).

✦ **For liquids**
Fill measuring cup to the brim.

◆ 불의 세기 Intensity of heat

**강불 [gangbul] / 센 불 [sen bul]
high heat**

Used when boiling liquids like soup, when bringing something to a boil, when quickly stir-frying ingredients, etc.

중불 [jungbul] medium heat

Used when heating a frying pan, when stir-frying or braising, etc.

약불 [yakppul] low heat

Used when applying heat for a long period of time, to give a deep taste to soups or when cooking hard vegetables, etc.; when shaping foods; and when foods need to be thoroughly steamed.

한식에 쓰이는 양념
LEARN BEFORE COOKING: BASIC KOREAN CONDIMENTS

간장 [ganjang]
soy sauce

된장 [doenjang]
doenjang (soybean paste)

고추장 [gochujang]
gochujang (red chili paste)

참기름 [chamgireum]
sesame oil

들기름 [deulgireum]
perilla oil

깨 [kkae]
sesame seeds

고춧가루 [gochutgaru]
red pepper powder

새우젓 [saeujeot]
salted shrimp

✦ **Different uses for different types of soy sauce**

- Korean-style soy sauce: soups, seasoned vegetables, etc.
- Brewed soy sauce: braised dishes, stir-fries, etc.
- Dark soy sauce: bulgogi, galbi, etc.

청양고추 [cheongyanggochu]
Cheongyang chili pepper

대파 [daepa]
green onion

마늘 [maneul]
garlic

Kimchi is the first Korean food that comes to mind, and is the representative, traditional fermented food of Korea. When people say "kimchi", we usually think of baechukimchi, but kimchi is actually a unique, fermented Korean food that can be made by pickling napa cabbage, radish, cucumbers, and other vegetables in salt, adding various seasonings (beginning with red pepper powder), mixing, and fermenting. Kimchi can be made with a variety of vegetables as the main ingredient, resulting in baechukimchi, kkakdugi (diced radish kimchi), Oisobagi (cucumber kimchi), yeolmukimchi (young summer radish kimchi), chonggak-kimchi (whole radish kimchi), gatkimchi (mustard leaf kimchi), and nabak-kimchi (water kimchi), each of which can come in very diverse forms.

배추김치 [baechugimchi]

Baechukimchi is what usually comes to mind when someone says "kimchi." A whole head of napa cabbage is cut into halves or quarters, pickled in salt water, and then a filling made of shredded radish and various seasonings is stuffed between the leaves before the cabbage is put into a container and left to ripen. When baechukimchi is made whole like this rather than cut, it's called "pogi kimchi". Pogi kimchi is usually made during gimjang for its long shelf life.

오이소박이 [oisobagi]

Kimchi made usually in the spring or summer by cutting into cucumbers, pickling them in salt, and filling the cuts with seasoned leeks.

총각김치 [chonggak-kkimchi]

The whole radish, including the leaves, is used for this kimchi, which is made by cutting the radish lengthwise into an appropriate size, pickling in salt, and mixing with various seasonings.

깍두기 [kkakttugi]

Kimchi made by dicing radishes into cubes, pickling in salt, and mixing with red pepper powder and other seasonings.

Rice, the representative staple crop of Koreans and a basic of Korean cooking, is made by washing dry rice three or four times, draining, then adding water and applying heat. When making rice in a rice pot (or ordinary pot) not only must the amount of water be controlled for, the heat must be carefully controlled as well in order to make sticky and delicious rice. But as electric rice cookers have become popular, today, you can make delicious rice, however, you want it just by adding the correct amount of water. It's standard to use only white rice when making rice, but people also add beans, red bean, barley, etc. to make multi-grain rice.

INGREDIENTS

2-3인분 Serves 2-3

2 cups of rice (non-glutinous)
2 ¼ cups of water

COOKING

PREPARATION

1

When cooking rice, water will increase the volume of dry rice by 1.2 times (or increase the weight by 1.5 times). For already soaked rice, water can be added in a 1:1 ratio.

2

When using an electric rice cooker, follow steps 1-3 and then cook the rice according to the directions for the rice cooker.

1. Put the rice in a bowl, and after pouring an adequate amount of water over the rice, mix quickly and then immediately drain out the water. With force, make a scrubbing motion in the rice to remove impurities on the surface of the rice. Repeat this 3 or 4 times until the water is clear, and then drain.

2. Add enough water to completely submerge the rice. In the summer, leave to soak for 30 minutes; in the winter, leave to soak for 2 hours.

3. Put the rice in a rice pot (or ordinary pot), add the correct amount of water, then boil over high heat. When the water begins to boil, reduce to medium heat and leave to boil for another 4-5 minutes, making sure it doesn't boil over.

4. Reduce the medium heat to low heat and thoroughly steam for 10-15 minutes until the level of the rice water subsides.

5. Turn off the heat. Leave to sit with the cover on for 5 minutes, then mix top and bottom well with a rice paddle.

KOREAN RECIPES

김치찌개
Kimchijjigae

⋆ KIMCHIJJIGAE ⋆

Kimchijjigae, as a stew made with fermented sour kimchi, is one of the most
common dishes added to a Korean table and is a typical kimchi-based food.
A dish once cooked by boiling kimchi made during winter gimjang into stew
in the spring when it had softened and become sour, with the development of
storage techniques, it has become a food that is eaten regardless of the season.
You can enjoy it in a variety of tastes depending on the ingredients you add,
such as pork, beef, anchovies, tuna, etc.

재료 INGREDIENTS

2-3인분 Serves 2-3

돼지고기 150g
150 grams of pork

배추김치 300g
300 grams of baechukimchi

대파 20g
20 grams of green onion

육수 또는 물 3컵
3 cups of stock or water

김치 국물 1/2컵
1/2 cup of kimchi juice

다진 마늘 1큰술 (15g)
1 tablespoon (15 grams) crushed garlic

식용유 1큰술
1 tablespoon cooking oil

◆━━ TIPS ━━◆

* Canned tuna, anchovies, etc. can be substituted for pork to suit your preferences.

* If you use rice water, anchovy stock, beef bone stock, etc. instead of water, the taste of the soup will become stronger. Rice water is the cloudy water that forms after washing rice, and is occasionally used as a stock in Korean food.

* Sour kimchi refers to kimchi that has been stored at a too-high temperature or for a long period of time so that it has over-ripened and has a sour taste.

준비 PREPARATION

◆ 찌개에 들어가는 돼지고기는 목살처럼 살과 지방이 같이 있는 부위로 준비한다.
Prepare a cut of pork that contains meat and fat together, such as pork shoulder, to put into the stew.

요리 COOKING

1 돼지고기는 두께 0.5cm 정도 크기로 썰고, 대파는 두께 0.5cm로 어슷썰기 한다.
Cut the pork into 0.5 cm thick pieces and slice the green onion diagonally into 0.5 cm thick pieces.

2 배추김치는 신김치로 준비하고, 포기김치의 경우는 3cm 정도로 썰어서 사용한다. 이미 썰어져 있는 막김치는 그대로 사용하면 된다.
Prepare sour baechukimchi, and if using a whole head of kimchi, cut into 3 cm pieces. Pre-cut easy kimchi can be used as is.

3 냄비에 식용유를 두르고 돼지고기를 2분 정도 볶다가 김치를 넣고 3~4분 정도 더 볶는다.
Add cooking oil to a pot and stir-fry the pork for about 2 minutes, then add the kimchi and continue to stir-fry for an additional 3-4 minutes.

4 돼지고기와 김치를 볶던 냄비에 물 3컵과 김치 국물 1/2컵을 넣고 같이 끓인다.
Add 3 cups of water and 1/2 cup of kimchi juice to the pot in which the pork and kimchi were stir-fried, and boil together.

5 센 불에서 끓이다가 국물이 한번 끓어 오르면 약불로 줄여 20분 이상 더 끓인다. 기호에 따라 소금이나 김치 국물로 간을 조절한다.
Boil over high heat and once the soup has risen to a boil, reduce to a low heat and boil for an additional 20 minutes. Adjust the taste with salt or kimchi juice according to your preferences.

6 찌개의 김치가 원하는 정도로 무르면 대파와 다진 마늘을 넣고 2분 정도 더 끓여 마무리한다.
When the kimchi in the stew is as soft as you would like it to be, add the green onion and crushed garlic and finish by boiling for an additional 2 minutes.

Track 001

재료 INGREDIENTS

배추김치 [baechugimchi]
baechukimchi

note
Baechukimchi is the most typical variety of kimchi, and when people say "kimchi," they are usually referring to baechukimchi.

목살 [mokssal]
pork shoulder

note
Compared to pork belly, this has less fat and more meat, and is often used in kimchijjigae, kimchijjim, etc.

Track 002

요리 COOKING

Base Form	Meaning	Examples
썰다 [sseolda]	to cut, to slice	• 파와 양파를 **써세요**. Slice the green onions and onions. • 포기김치를 **썰어서** 사용하세요. Cut and use the head of kimchi.
끓이다 [kkeurida]	to boil	• 다시마를 넣고 육수를 **끓이세요**. Add kelp and boil the stock. • 센 불에서 **끓이다가** 약불로 줄이세요. Boil over high heat and then reduce to low heat.
무르다 [mureuda]	to soften	• 돼지고기가 **물렀어요**. The pork has softened. • 김치가 **무르면** 파를 넣으세요. Once the kimchi has softened, add the green onions.

Let's Speak Korean!

━○ 안녕하세요?

Track 003

A 안녕하세요? 잘 지냈어요? Hello. Are you doing well?

B 네, 잘 지냈어요. Yes, I'm doing well.

안녕하세요? is a greeting without formality that can be used when you meet anyone, regardless of the time of day or your relationship. In comparison, 안녕하십니까? is a polite greeting, and you can use 안녕 with friends or those who are of lower rank than you.

A **안녕하십니까? / 안녕?** Hello.

B **안녕하십니까? / 안녕?** Hello.

━○ 김치찌개입니다.

Track 004

A 이게 김치찌개입니까? Is this kimchijjigae?

B 네, 김치찌개입니다. Yes, it's kimchijjigae.

입니다 is honorific and used in the form of "N + 입니다" with objects, a person's name, a nationality, etc. 입니까? is the interrogative form. 이게 is a shortened form of 이것 and means "this."

A **배추김치입니까?** Is this baechukimchi?

한국 사람   김민호

B **네, 배추김치입니다.** Yes, it's baechukimchi.

한국 사람   김민호

김치볶음밥
Kimchi-bokkeumbap

• KIMCHI-BOKKEUMBAP •

Kimchi-bokkeumbap is a fried rice dish made with sliced kimchi and steamed rice, or with added ham, sausage, etc. It is a dish created when frying pans were introduced to Korea, and can be made into a wonderful bowl of food with only kimchi and rice. Of the different varieties of kimchi, baechukimchi is usually used, and these days, it is also made with kkakdugi cut into small pieces. It can be eaten with a fried egg, cheese, etc. on top.

재료 INGREDIENTS

2인분 Serves 2

배추김치 300g
300 grams of baechukimchi

밥 2공기 (400g)
2 bowls (400 grams) of steamed rice

소시지 120g
120 grams of sausage

달걀 2개
2 eggs

김치 국물 3큰술
3 tablespoons kimchi juice

식용유 2큰술
2 tablespoons cooking oil

준비 PREPARATION

◆ 밥은 따뜻하거나 차갑거나 상관없으며, 즉석밥을 이용할 경우는 전자레인지 등을 활용하여 미리 조리해 둔다.
Rice can be used warm or cold, and if using instant rice, prepare beforehand in the microwave, etc.

요리 COOKING

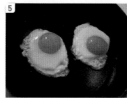

1 김치는 1×1.5cm 정도의 크기로 자르고, 햄이나 소시지는 얇게 김치 크기와 비슷하게 자른다.
Cut the kimchi into 1x1.5 cm pieces and cut the ham or sausage into thin pieces the same size as the kimchi.

2 팬을 달구어 중불로 줄이고 식용유를 두르고, 햄 또는 소시지를 먼저 볶는다.
Heat the pan and reduce to medium heat, coat with cooking oil, and stir-fry the ham or sausage first.

3 소시지가 절반 정도 익었을 때 김치를 넣고 중간 불에서 2분 정도 볶는다.
When the sausage is halfway cooked, add the kimchi and stir-fry over medium heat for 2 minutes.

4 김치가 완전히 익으면 밥을 넣고 뭉치지 않도록 섞어가며 볶는다. 부족한 간은 김치 국물이나 소금, 간장을 활용하여 기호에 맞게 조절한다.
When the kimchi is fully cooked, add the rice and stir-fry while mixing so as not to clump together. If the flavor is insufficient, adjust using kimchi juice, salt, or soy sauce to suit your preferences.

5 노른자가 살짝 익을 정도의 반숙 달걀 프라이를 만든다.
Prepare an egg sunny side up.

6 볶음밥이 완성되면 그릇에 담고 달걀 프라이를 밥 위에 얹어 곁들인다.
When the bokkeumbap is finished, put in a bowl and top with the fried egg.

TIPS

* Sour kimchi should be used for the best taste; kimchi becomes sour kimchi after 1-2 days at room temperature. If you use less aged kimchi as is, it will be less tasty.

* If using kkakdugi instead of baechukimchi, you should cut well-fermented kkakdugi into small pieces so it can be stir-fried well with the rice for the best taste.

재료 INGREDIENTS

밥 [bap]
rice

note
Rice is the basis of a Korean meal, and this table setting is completed by adding soup and side dishes centered around the rice.

깍두기 [kkakttugi]
kkakdugi

note
As a type of kimchi made with radish, this goes well with seolleongtang (ox bone soup), galbitang (short rib soup), etc.

요리 COOKING

Base Form	Meaning	Examples
볶다 [boktta]	to stir-fry	• 소시지를 **볶다가** 김치를 넣으세요. Stir-fry the sausage and then add the kimchi. • 김치가 익으면 밥을 넣고 **볶으세요.** When the kimchi has cooked, add the rice and stir-fry.
달구다 [dalguda]	to heat (up)	• 먼저 프라이팬을 **달구세요.** First heat the frying pan. • 팬이 **달궈지면** 기름을 넣으세요. When the pan is heated, add the oil.
담다 [damtta]	to put something (in/on something)	• 김치볶음밥을 그릇에 **담아요.** Put the kimchi-bokkeumbap in a bowl. • 반찬을 접시에 **담아** 주세요. Put the side dishes on a plate.

Let's Speak Korean!

—○ 김치찌개가 아닙니다.

A 이게 김치찌개입니까? Is this kimchijjigae?

B 아니요, 김치찌개가 아닙니다. No, it's not kimchijjigae.
김치볶음밥입니다. It's kimchi-bokkeumbap.

The 가 added after 김치찌개 is a subject marker. When the preceding word ends in a consonant, the subject marker 이 is added, and when it ends in a vowel, 가 is added. "N + 이/가 아닙니다" expresses the negative meaning of "N + 입니다."

Final consonant O + 이: 갈비탕이	찜닭이
Final consonant X + 가: 김치가	깍두기가

A 이게 김치볶음밥입니까? Is this kimchi-bokkeumbap?

갈비탕	찜닭	김치	깍두기

B 아니요, 김치볶음밥이 아닙니다. No, it's not kimchi-bokkeumbap.

갈비탕이	찜닭이	김치가	깍두기가

—○ 그게 김치입니다.

A 이게 김치입니까? Is this kimchi?

B 네, 그게 김치입니다. Yes, that's kimchi.

이게, 그게, and 저게 are the shortened forms of 이것이, 그것이, and 저것이, which are 이것, 그것, and 저것 with the subject marker 이 added on. 이것 is used to indicate an item close to the speaker, 그것 for an object close to the listener, and 저것 for an object far from both parties.

A 이게 불고기입니까? Is this bulgogi?   **B** 네, 그게 불고기입니다. Yes, that's bulgogi.

그게	저게

이게	저게

김치전

Kimchijeon

• KIMCHIJEON •

Kimchijeon is a type of jeon (pancake) made by finely chopping kimchi, adding it into a flour batter, and frying it until sizzling in a frying pan. Along with kimchijjigae and kimchi-bokkeumbap, kimchijeon is a typical kimchi-based food. Often eaten as a snack, it can also be enjoyed as a side dish or served with alcohol. If you put additional ingredients that go well with kimchi, such as squid, shrimp, and other seafood, or ham, sausage, etc., you can make special types of kimchijeon.

재료 INGREDIENTS

2-3인분 Serves 2-3

배추김치 300g
300 grams of baechukimchi

밀가루 3컵
3 cups of flour

물 2½컵
2½ cups of water

김치 국물 1/2컵
1/2 cup of kimchi juice

햄 또는 소시지 100g
100 grams of ham or sausage

식용유 1/2컵
1/2 cup of cooking oil

* Sour kimchi should be used for a better flavor.

준비 PREPARATION

◆ 햄 대신 소시지를 넣어도 되며 얇게 썰어야 한다. 소시지나 햄의 짠맛이 너무 강할 경우에는 끓는 물에 한 번 데쳐서 사용한다.
Sausage can be added instead of ham, but should be thinly sliced. If the salty taste of the sausage or ham is too strong, blanch once in boiling water before using.

요리 COOKING

1 배추김치는 1×1.5cm 정도 크기로 썬다. 소시지나 햄은 김치와 비슷한 크기로 얇게 썬다.
Cut baechukimchi into 1×1.5 cm pieces. Cut sausage or ham thinly into pieces the same size as the kimchi.

2 볼에 밀가루와 물, 김치 국물을 넣고 밀가루가 보이지 않게 섞는다.
Put flour, water, and kimchi juice in a bowl, and mix until flour cannot be seen.

3 밀가루 반죽에 김치와 소시지나 햄을 넣는다. 팬을 달구어 중약불로 줄인다.
Add the kimchi and sausage or ham to the flour batter. Heat a pan and reduce heat to medium-low.

4 팬에 식용유를 1큰술 정도 두르고 팬의 크기에 따라 반죽을 한 국자쯤 넣어 얇게 편다.
Coat the pan with about 1 tablespoon of cooking oil, add about 1 ladle of batter depending on the size of the pan, and spread it thin.

5 윗부분이 절반 정도 익으면 뒤집는다.
Flip when the top part is about halfway cooked.

6 타지 않도록 여러 번 뒤집으며 앞뒤로 노릇노릇하게 지진다.
Flip several times to avoid burning until top and bottom are fried golden brown.

Vocabulary

Track 009

재료 INGREDIENTS

밀가루 [milkkaru]
flour

note

All-purpose flour is usually used for kimchijeon.

식용유 [sigyongnyu]
cooking oil

note

Any vegetable oil used in cooking is called "cooking oil," but in Korean food, "cooking oil" usually refers to soybean oil. Grapeseed oil, corn oil, olive oil, etc. are also used.

Track 010

요리 COOKING

Base Form	Meaning	Examples
넣다 [neota]	to add	• 반죽에 소시지와 김치를 **넣으세요.** Add the sausage and kimchi to the batter. • 국물을 **넣고** 골고루 섞으세요. Add the broth and mix evenly.
섞다 [seoktta]	to mix	• 밀가루를 넣고 **섞어서** 반죽을 만드세요. Add the flour and mix to make the batter. • 반죽이 뭉치지 않게 **섞으세요.** Mix so that the dough does not clump.
지지다 [jijida]	to fry	• 앞뒤로 노릇하게 **지지세요.** Fry the top and bottom to golden brown. • 두부를 기름에 **지지면** 맛있어요. If you fry tofu in oil, it tastes good.

Let's Speak Korean!

🔑 밀가루예요.

Track 011

A 이거 밀가루예요? Is this flour?

B 네, 밀가루예요. Yes, it's flour.

예요 has the same meaning as "to be," and is added after a noun that has a final syllable ending in a vowel. If a question mark (?) is added after 예요, it becomes an interrogative, and if a period (.) is added, it becomes a declarative.

Final consonant X + 예요: 밀가루예요   식용유예요   김치예요

A 저게 식용유예요? Is this cooking oil?

김치   갈비

B 네, 식용유예요. Yes, it's cooking oil.

김치   갈비

🔑 김치전이에요.

Track 012

A 이거 피자예요? Is this pizza?

B 아니요, 김치전이에요. No, it's kimchijeon.

Like 예요, 이에요 means "to be," and is added after a noun that has a final syllable ending in a consonant. If a question mark (?) is added after 이에요, it becomes an interrogative, and if a period (.) is added, it becomes a declarative.

Final consonant O + 이에요: 김밥이에요   갈비찜이에요

A 그게 김밥이에요? Is that gimbap?

갈비찜   해물파전

B 네, 김밥이에요. Yes, it's gimbap.

갈비찜   해물파전

김치찜
Kimchijjim

• KIMCHIJJIM •

Kimchijjim is a steamed dish cooked by adding thick pork to aged or sour kimchi and boiling it down. Because it is boiled for a long time over low heat, the kimchi and pork become very soft, and the taste of the broth, which goes well with these two ingredients, is also excellent. The ingredients are almost the same as those for kimchijjigae with pork, but this is among the main dishes that contain less broth and more pork.

재료 INGREDIENTS

2-3인분 Serves 2-3

배추김치 550g
550 grams of baechukimchi

돼지고기 (목살) 450g
450 grams of pork (pork shoulder)

양파 1/2개
1/2 onion

대파 1/2대
1/2 green onion

청양고추 1개
1 Cheongyang chili pepper

설탕 1/2큰술
1/2 tablespoon sugar

간장 1큰술
1 tablespoon soy sauce

다진 마늘 1큰술
1 tablespoon crushed garlic

고춧가루 1큰술
1 tablespoon red pepper powder

육수 4컵
4 cups of stock

◀ TIPS ▶

* Cheongyang chili pepper can be omitted if desired.

* Aged or sour kimchi must be used for kimchi-jjim. Prepare a head of kimchi that hasn't been cut into small pieces.

* Mugeunji ("aged kim-chi") refers to gimjang kimchi that has fermented for longer than sour kimchi.

준비 PREPARATION

◆ 육수는 다시마와 멸치를 넣고 국물이 끓으면 약불로 20분 이상 끓여 준비한다.
Prepare the stock by adding kelp and anchovies, and once it comes to a boil, continue to boil over low heat for at least 20 minutes.

◆ 돼지고기는 어떤 부위든 괜찮지만, 지방이 조금 섞여 있어야 고기가 잘 무른다.
Any cut of pork is fine, but the meat should have some fat mixed in for it to soften well.

요리 COOKING

1 돼지고기는 두툼하게 큰 덩어리로 썰고, 김치는 세로로 2등분 한다.
Cut the pork into thick chunks and cut the kimchi vertically into 2 halves.

2 양파는 굵게 채 썰고, 대파와 청양고추는 어슷하게 썬다.
Shred the onion into thick pieces and slice the green onion and Cheongyang chili pepper diagonally.

3 냄비에 김치를 반으로 나누어 김치 – 돼지고기 – 김치의 순서로 포개서 넣고, 양파와 청양고추도 넣는다.
Divide the kimchi in half and add to the pot in layers in the order of kimchi-pork-kimchi, then add the onion and Cheongyang chili pepper.

4 육수를 넣고 설탕, 간장, 다진 마늘, 고춧가루를 모두 넣고 잘 섞어 준다.
Add the broth, then add the sugar, soy sauce, crushed garlic, and red pepper powder and mix well.

5 센 불로 끓이다가 국물이 끓으면 중약불로 줄여 1시간 정도 고기와 김치가 완전히 무를 때까지 끓인다.
Boil over high heat, and once the soup boils, reduce to medium-low heat and continue to boil for about an hour until the meat and kimchi have completely softened.

6 마지막으로 김치와 고기가 무르면 대파를 넣고 기호에 따라 소금으로 간을 더하여 5분 정도 더 끓여 완성한다.
Finally, when the kimchi and meat have softened, add the green onion, salt according to your preferences to increase the taste, and complete by boiling for an additional 5 minutes.

Vocabulary

재료 INGREDIENTS

청양고추 [cheongyang-gochu]
Cheongyang chili pepper

note
Cheongyang chili peppers have a very strong spicy taste. They are usually sliced diagonally and used to add more spice to a dish.

마늘 [maneul]
garlic

note
Garlic is a spice that is essentially used in almost every Korean food. When raw, the taste and fragrance are strong, but when cooked, the fragrance and spicy flavor are weakened.

요리 COOKING

Base Form	Meaning	Examples
굵다 [guktta]	to be thick, to be bulky	• 감자가 아주 **굵어요**. Potatoes are very bulky. • 양파는 **굵게** 채 썬다. Shred the onion into thick pieces.
켜다 [kyeoda]	to turn on	• 가스레인지에 불을 **켜세요**. Turn on the fire of the gas stove. • 불을 **켜고** 끓이세요. Turn on the heat and boil.
줄이다 [jurida]	to reduce	• 불을 **줄이고** 약불에서 2분 끓이세요. Reduce the heat and boil for 2 minutes over low heat. • 매우면 고춧가루 양을 **줄이세요**. If it's spicy, reduce the amount of red pepper powder.

Let's Speak Korean!

─○ 이 음식은 김치찜이에요.

Track 015

A 이 음식 이름이 뭐예요? What's the name of this food?

B 이 음식은 김치찜이에요. This food is kimchijjim.

은/는 is a postpositional particle added after a word that indicates the topic. If the preceding word ends in a consonant, 은 is used, and if it ends in a vowel, 는 is used. 은/는, as a postpositional particle indicating the topic, is used instead of the subject marker 이/가.

> Final consonant O + 은: 마늘은   이름은
> Final consonant X + 는: 돼지고기는   청양고추는

Exercise

✦ 돼지고기는 크게 썹니다. Cut the pork into large pieces.

✦ 청양고추는 어슷하게 썹니다. Slice the Cheongyang chili pepper diagonally.

✦ 마늘은 다집니다. Crush the garlic.

✦ 음식 이름은 김치찜입니다. This dish's name is kimchijjim.

─○ 오늘 메뉴가 뭐예요?

Track 016

A 오늘 메뉴가 뭐예요? What's on the menu today?

B 김치전이에요. It's kimchijeon.

The 뭐 in 뭐예요? means "what," making 뭐예요? mean "what is ~?".

Exercise

A 이 음식이 뭐예요? What is this dish?

B 김치찜이에요. It's kimchijjim.

> 불고기   삼계탕

배추김치
Baechukimchi

• BAECHUKIMCHI •

This is a fermented food made by pickling napa cabbage in salt and stuffing it with a filling made of red pepper powder, shredded radish, green onion, garlic, salted seafood, etc., or mixing it with a seasoning made of red pepper powder, green onion, garlic, salted seafood, etc. Baechukimchi is a typical Korean food and an essential side dish at a Korean table setting. In Korea, there is a culture of "gimjang," in which large quantities of kimchi are made and stored before the cold winter arrives.

STEPS OF MAKING BAECHUKIMCHI

PICKLING → **MAKING** → **FERMENTING**

절이기 PICKLING

재료 INGREDIENTS

배추 1포기 (3kg)
1 head (3 kilograms) of napa cabbage

소금 300g
300 grams of salt

물 2리터
2 liters of water

큰 그릇
a large bowl (large enough to fit a head of cabbage)

TIPS

* Sun-dried salt is recommended, but if none is available, use a coarse grain salt.

* As the weight of a head of napa cabbage varies, prepare 100 grams of salt per 1 kilogram of napa cabbage.

* The curing time for napa cabbage differs depending on the water content of the napa cabbage, the air temperature, and the concentration of the salt water. When you try to fold the stems of the napa cabbage, if they fold gently, then the napa cabbage is well pickled.

1 배추는 밑동을 잘라내고 겉잎은 뜯어낸다.
Cut off the base of the napa cabbage and remove the outer leaves.

2 배추 크기에 따라 세로로 2등분 또는 4등분으로 자른다.
Depending on the size of the napa cabbage, cut vertically into 2 or 4.

3 큰 그릇에 물과 소금 절반을 넣고 완전히 녹인다.
In a large bowl, add water and half of the salt, and dissolve completely.

4 자른 배추를 소금물에 골고루 적시고, 줄기 사이사이에 소금을 뿌려 4–5시간쯤 절인다.
Steep the cut napa cabbage evenly in the salt water, sprinkle salt between the stems (the white center of the leaves), and pickle about 4-5 hours.

5 30분 정도 간격으로 배추를 뒤집어 준다.
Turn the napa cabbage over at 30-minute intervals.

6 절여진 배추를 찬물에 3번 헹궈 물기를 뺀다.
Rinse the pickled napa cabbage 3 times in cold water and drain.

재료 INGREDIENTS

찹쌀가루 (또는 밀가루)
3큰술
3 tablespoons glutinous rice flour
(or wheat flour)

물 2컵
2 cups of water

1 냄비에 찹쌀가루를 넣고 물을 조금씩 넣으며 찹쌀가루가 뭉치지 않게 잘 풀어 준다.
Put glutinous rice flour in a pot, add water little by little, and loosen to remove clumps.

2 약불에서 계속 저어 주며, 5분쯤 지나서 점성이 생기면 불을 끄고 식혀 준다.
Stir continuously over low heat, and after 5 minutes, when it becomes viscous, turn off the heat and allow to cool.

재료 INGREDIENTS

양파 1
1 onion

사과 (또는 배) 1/4개
1/4 apple (or pear)

고춧가루 1½컵
1½ cups of red pepper powder

액젓 1/2컵
1/2 cup of fish sauce

새우젓 2큰술
2 tablespoons salted shrimp

설탕 1큰술
1 tablespoon sugar

마늘 15개
15 cloves of garlic

생강 15g
15 grams of ginger

1 믹서기에 큼직하게 자른 사과와 양파 그리고 마늘, 생강, 설탕, 새우젓, 액젓을 모두 넣고 갈아 준다.
In a blender, add the roughly cut apple and onion as well as the garlic, ginger, sugar, salted shrimp, and fish sauce, and blend.

2 식혀 놓은 찹쌀 풀과 고춧가루, **1**의 갈아 둔 양념을 골고루 섞어 준다.
Add the cooled glutinous rice paste and red pepper powder to the blended seasoning from step 1 and mix evenly.

TIPS

If salted shrimp is not available, increase fish sauce by 2/3 and add salt to taste.

만들기 3 MAKING 3 | 김치소 넣기 ADDING THE KIMCHI FILLING

재료 INGREDIENTS

절인 배추
salted napa cabbage

무 600g
600 grams of radish

쪽파 15개
15 scallions

◄ TIPS ►

* Prepare in a ratio of 200 grams of radish to 1 kilogram of napa cabbage, and adjust according to your preferences.

* The taste may differ depending on how pickled the napa cabbage is, so taste a stem with some of the filling before adding the filling to the whole napa cabbage, and add salt to the filling to suit your tastes.

* If the kimchi does not have enough juice, put the kimchi whole into a container, add 1 cup of water and a pinch of salt to the bowl in which the seasoning was mixed to make kimchi juice with the remaining seasoning, and pour it over the kimchi.

1 무는 4-5cm 크기로 얇게 채썰기 한다.
Shred the radish into thin 4-5 cm pieces.

2 쪽파는 4-5cm 크기로 썰고, 대파를 사용할 때에는 같은 크기로 어슷썰기 한다.
Slice the scallions into 4-5 cm pieces, and if using green onion, slice diagonally to the same size.

3 만들어 놓은 양념에 쪽파와 무를 넣고 버무려서 김치소를 만든다.
Add the scallions and radish to the seasoning and mix to make the kimchi filling.

4 절인 배추의 줄기 사이사이에 김치소를 바르듯이 넣고 마지막에 겉잎으로 배추 전체를 감싼다.
Add the kimchi filling as if spreading it between the stems of the pickled napa cabbage and then finish by wrapping the entire napa cabbage with the outer leaves.

숙성하기 FERMENTING

✦ 김치소를 넣은 김치를 안쪽이 위로 향하도록 통에 담고 절인 배추 겉잎으로 덮은 뒤 눌러 준다. 김치는 20℃ 정도의 상온에서 하루 정도 지나면 숙성이 된다. 숙성 후에는 냉장고에 보관한다.
Put the kimchi with the kimchi filling in a container with the inside facing up, cover it with pickled napa cabbage leaves, and press. The kimchi will ripen when at room temperature of about 20 degrees Celsius for around one day. Store in the refrigerator after fermenting.

Track 017

재료 INGREDIENTS

배추 [baechu]
napa cabbage

note
This is one of Korea's 4 major vegetables and the main ingredient in kimchi. In addition to kimchi, it is also used to make side dishes of soups or seasoned vegetables.

고춧가루 [gochutkkaru]
red pepper powder

note
Ripe peppers are dried and ground up into an indispensible seasoning ingredient in Korean food. This is used to make red pepper paste, or in kimchi or various other Korean foods.

Track 018

요리 COOKING

Base Form	Meaning	Examples
절이다 [jeorida]	to salt, to pickle	• 배추를 4–5시간 정도 **절이세요**. Pickle the napa cabbage for around 4-5 hours. • 새우젓은 소금에 **절인** 음식이에요. Salted shrimp is a food pickled in salt.
자르다 [jareuda]	to cut	• 배추를 **자르세요**. Cut the napa cabbage. • **자른** 감자와 대파를 넣으세요. Add the chopped potatoes and green onion.
끄다 [kkeuda]	to turn off	• 5분 후에 불을 **끄고** 식히세요. After 5 minutes, turn off the heat and leave to cool. • 무와 고기가 익으면 불을 **끄세요**. Once the radish and meat have cooked, turn off the heat.

Let's Speak Korean!

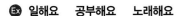 요리해요.

 Track 019

A 뭐 해요?   What are you doing?

B 요리해요.   I'm cooking.

해요 is a form of the verb 하다 with the word ending −여요 attached, and 해요? is the interrogative form. 해요 can be used alone or combined with some nouns in the form of "N + 해요" to be used as a verb.

(Ex) 일**해요**   공부**해요**   노래**해요**

A 뭐 해요? What are you doing?

B 한국어 공부해요. I'm studying Korean.

> 일하다   노래하다   운동하다

  언제 해요?

 Track 020

A 김장은 언제 해요?   When do you do gimjang?

B 오늘 해요.   I'm doing it today.

언제 is an interrogative that asks for a time, and the answer to the question 언제 해요? can be made by putting a word that expresses time in the place of 언제.

(Ex) 내일 해요.   지금 해요.   다음 주에 해요.

A 한국에 언제 가요? When are you going to Korea?

B 내일 가요. I'm going tomorrow.

> 지금   다음 주에

떡꼬치
Tteok-kkochi

• TTEOK-KKOCHI •

Tteok-kkochi is a food made by skewering tteokbokkitteok (rice cakes) in parallel and frying or grilling in a pan with plenty of oil, and is eaten with sauce spread on top. Unlike tteokbokki, the outside is crispy and the inside is chewy. Because it is fried or grilled in oil, it is savory, and because of the sauce made of a mix of gochujang and ketchup, you can taste spicy and sweet flavors at the same time. Along with tteokbokki, it is a famous street food, and these days, is often eaten at home as a snack as well.

재료 INGREDIENTS

2-3인분 Serves 2-3

떡볶이떡 (가래떡) 250g
250 grams of tteokbokkitteok
(or garaetteok)

소시지 5-7개
5-7 sausages

나무 꼬치 10개
10 wooden skewers

식용유
cooking oil

Sauce & Marinade

고추장 1/3큰술
1/3 tablespoon gochujang

간장 1큰술
1 tablespoon soy sauce

설탕 3큰술
3 tablespoons sugar

케첩 2큰술
2 tablespoons ketchup

물 50ml
50 milliliters of water

준비 PREPARATION

◆ 떡은 냉동 제품을 사용해도 되며, 가래떡은 5-7cm 정도로 잘라서 준비한다.
You can use frozen tteok or prepare garaetteok by cutting it into 5-7 cm long pieces.

◆ 소시지는 떡과 비슷한 길이로 잘라서 준비한다.
Prepare the sausage by cutting to a similar size as the tteok.

요리 COOKING

1 떡이 많이 굳어 있거나 냉동 떡인 경우는 끓는 물에 2-3분 정도 데쳐서 물기를 제거한다.
If the tteok is hard or if using frozen tteok, blanch for 2-3 minutes in boiling water and then drain.

2 소시지는 윗면이나 옆면에 살짝 칼집을 낸다.
Make small cuts to the top or side of the sausage.

3 꼬치에 떡만 꽂거나 떡과 소시지를 번갈아 가면서 꽂는다.
Put the tteok alone or alternating with sausage on the skewers.

4 팬이나 작은 냄비에 소스 재료를 모두 넣고 끓기 시작하면 불을 끈다.
Put all the ingredients for the sauce in a pan or small pot and turn off the heat once they start to boil.

5 팬에 기름을 넉넉하게 두르고 꼬치를 노릇하게 구운 뒤 기름을 뺀다. 섭씨 190도에서 1-2분 정도 튀겨도 된다.
Coat the pan with plenty of oil, then remove the oil after pan-frying the skewers to golden brown. You can also fry at 190 degrees Celsius for 1-2 minutes.

6 구운 꼬치에 소스를 골고루 바른다. 땅콩이나 잣 등 견과류가 있으면 작게 다져 위에 뿌려 준다.
Spread the sauce evenly on the pan-fried skewers. If you have nuts such as peanuts, pine nuts, etc., chop into small pieces and sprinkle on top.

Vocabulary

Track 021

재료 INGREDIENTS

가래떡 [garaetteok]
garaetteok

note

Garaetteok is named for its long shape. It's eaten as is, but is cut diagonally and boiled in tteokguk on the morning of Seollal, the lunar new year.

설탕 [seoltang]
sugar

note

Sugar is not only used to give a sweet taste to foods, but also added to meat before cooking to tenderize it, or used to give a gloss to other foods. White sugar is usually used in Korean foods, while dark brown sugar is used in Korean sweets such as yaksik, sujeonggwa, hotteok, etc.

Track 022

요리 COOKING

Base Form	Meaning	Examples
많다 [manta]	to be a lot, very	• 맛있는 음식이 **많아요**. There is a lot of delicious food. • 떡이 **많이** 굳어 있어요. The tteok is very hard.
있다 [it-tta]	to be, to have	• 땅콩이 **있으면** 뿌리세요. If you have peanuts, sprinkle them on top. • 냉장고에 김치가 **있어요**. There is kimchi in the fridge.
작다 [jaktta]	to be small	• 냄비가 너무 **작아요**. The pot is too small. • 땅콩을 **작게** 다지세요. Chop the peanuts into small pieces.

Let's Speak Korean!

─○ 떡볶이하고 달라요.

Track 023

A 이거 떡볶이예요? Is this tteokbokki?

B 아니요, 떡볶이하고 달라요. No, this is different from tteokbokki.

The 하고 in "N + 하고 다르다" is a postpositional particle that indicates an object being compared with something else or set as a standard. It has a different meaning from "N₁ + 하고 N₂."

Ex 김치찌개하고 달라요.
달걀하고 같아요.

Exercise

✦ 닭갈비는 닭볶음탕하고 같아요? Is dakgalbi the same as dakbokkeumtang?

✦ 달걀은 계란하고 같아요. Dalgyal is the same as gyeran.

✦ 겉절이는 배추김치하고 달라요. Geotjeori is different from baechukimchi.

Be careful!
When 다르다 is attached to an ending that begins with a vowel, the ㄹ in the stem changes to ㄹㄹ.

─○ 정말 맛있네요.

Track 024

A 소스를 발라서 먹어 보세요. Try spreading sauce on and eating this.

B 네, 정말 맛있네요. Yes, it certainly is delicious.

–네요 is a sentence final ending that indicates amazement at a thought or feeling. It is used in the form of "V/A + –네요."

Ex 요리하(다) + 네요 → 요리하네요   끓(다) + 네요 → 끓네요
맛있(다) + 네요 → 맛있네요   많(다) + 네요 → 많네요

Exercise

A 떡꼬치 좀 드셔 보세요. Try some tteok-kkochi.

B 네, 맛있네요. Yes, it certainly is delicious.

| 크기가 작다 | 양이 많다 | 맵다 | 짜다 |

떡볶이
Tteokbokki

• TTEOKBOKKI •

Tteokbokki is a spicy food made by cutting garaetteok into
bite-sized pieces or by using tteokbokkitteok and boiling with gochujang,
eomuk, etc. The chewy tteok is even more delicious when dipped
into the plentiful sweet and spicy sauce. Tteokbokki is a typical
street food, and goes well with the fried food and sundae sold with it.
Tteokbokkitteok can be made of rice or wheat, which you can
choose depending on your preferences.

재료 INGREDIENTS

2-3인분 Serves 2-3

떡볶이떡 400g
400 grams of tteokbokkitteok

어묵 2-3장 (160g)
2-3 sheets (160 grams) of eomuk

대파 30g
30 grams of green onion

고추장 1큰술
1 tablespoon gochujang

간장 1/2큰술
1/2 tablespoon soy sauce

고춧가루 1/2큰술
1/2 tablespoon red pepper powder

설탕 1큰술
1 tablespoon sugar

물 500ml
500 milliliters of water

육수 만들기 MAKING STOCK

물 600-700ml에 다시마, 국물용 멸치, 대파, 양파 등을 넣고 센 불에 올려 끓어오르면 약불로 줄여 10-15분쯤 끓인다.
Add kelp, anchovies for soup, green onion, white onion, etc. to 600-700 ml of water and bring to a boil over high heat, then reduce heat to low and boil for about 10-15 minutes.

⬦ TIPS ⬦

* This is even more delicious when made with anchovy or kelp stock instead of water.

* It tastes good with added hard-boiled eggs or cabbage.

준비 PREPARATION

◆ 떡은 기호에 따라 밀떡 또는 쌀떡을 준비하고 물에 헹구어 둔다.
Prepare tteok made of wheat or rice depending on your preferences, rinse them in water, and let them sit.

◆ 양배추 등 다른 채소를 더 넣거나, 떡볶이 국물과 튀김 등을 같이 먹으려면 국물을 넉넉하게 넣는다.
If adding cabbage and other vegetables or eating with fried foods, prepare a generous amount of broth.

요리 COOKING

1 떡볶이떡은 찬물에 10분 정도 담가 둔다.
Soak the tteokbokkitteok in cold water for 10 minutes.

2 대파는 어슷썰기 하고 어묵은 떡볶이와 비슷한 크기로 썬다.
Slice the green onion diagonally and cut the eomuk into pieces a similar size as the tteok.

3 깊은 프라이팬이나 냄비에 물이나 육수를 붓고 고추장, 고춧가루, 설탕을 넣고 끓인다.
Pour the water or broth into a deep frying pan or pot, add the gochujang, red pepper powder, and sugar, and boil.

4 국물이 끓으면 떡과 어묵을 넣고 부족한 간은 간장을 추가한다.
Once the sauce boils, add the eomuk, and add soy sauce if the flavor is insufficient.

5 약불에서 국물의 양이 원하는 정도로 걸쭉하게 졸아들 때까지 끓인다.
Boil over low heat until the sauce has thickened and reduced to the desired amount.

6 국물의 양이 원하는 정도가 되면 대파를 넣고 완성한다.
When the sauce has reached the desired amount, add the green onion and complete.

Vocabulary

Track 025

재료 INGREDIENTS

떡볶이떡 [tteokbokkitteok]
tteokbokkitteok

note
Tteokbokkitteok is garaetteok made thin and short so that It is suitable for tteokbokki. It can also be made of wheat instead of rice.

다시마 [dasima]
kelp

note
Kelp is often used along with shiitake mushrooms, radish, etc. to make stock for soups, but can also be eaten fried or as a ssam (vegetable for wraps).

Track 026

요리 COOKING

Base Form	Meaning	Examples
맛있다 [masit-tta]/ [madit-tta]	to be delicious, to taste good	• 삶은 달걀을 넣어도 **맛있어요.** It tastes good if hard-boiled eggs are added, too. • **맛있는** 음식을 먹고 싶어요. I want to eat delicious food.
비슷하다 [biseutada]	to be similar	• 떡을 크기가 **비슷하게** 써세요. Cut the tteok to a similar size. • 떡꼬치와 떡볶이의 재료는 **비슷해요.** The ingredients for tteok-kkochi and tteokbokki are similar.
넉넉하다 [neongneokada]	to be plenty, to be enough	• 국물을 **넉넉하게** 넣으세요. Add plenty of sauce. • 5인분을 만들기에 재료는 **넉넉해요.** The ingredients are enough to cook for five people.

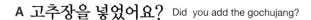

Let's Speak Korean!

─● 고추장을 넣었어요.

 Track 027

A 고추장을 넣었어요? Did you add the gochujang?

B 네, 고추장을 넣었어요. Yes, I added the gochujang.

–았/었– is a past tense pre-final ending used to express the finished state of a movement or condition.

> V/A stem with ㅏ/ㅗ + –았어요: 작(다) + 았어요 → 작았어요
>
> V/A stem with other vowels + –었어요: 넣(다) +었어요 → 넣었어요
>
> 하다 → 했어요: 요리하(다) → 요리했어요

Exercise

+ 달걀을 삶았어요. I boiled the eggs.
+ 파를 썰었어요. I cut the green onion.
+ 재료를 추가했어요. I added the ingredients.

─● 고추장 때문에 매워요.

 Track 028

A 괜찮아요? Is it all right?

B 고추장 때문에 매워요. It's spicy because of the gochujang.

때문에 is used in the form of N 때문에 to indicate that a person or object is the reason for or cause of something.

Ex 설탕 때문에   고춧가루 때문에

Exercise

A 맛있어요? Is it delicious?

B 네, 김치 때문에 더 맛있어요. Yes, it's more delicious because of the kimchi.

| 고춧가루 | 설탕 | 식초 |

궁중떡볶이
Gungjungtteokbokki

• GUNGJUNGTTEOKBOKKI •

A fried food made by cutting garaetteok into bite-sized pieces, adding
beef, shiitake mushrooms, etc., and seasoning with soy sauce and sesame oil.
As it was enjoyed in the royal palace since ancient times, it is called
gungjungtteokbokki (meaning "royal palace tteokbokki"), and also
ganjangtteokbokki as it is made with soy sauce instead of gochujang.
It is not spicy, and the tastes of the tteok, beef, and mushrooms stir-fried in soy
sauce harmonize together. These days, it is enjoyed even more
by adding bell peppers, carrots, etc.

재료 INGREDIENTS

2-3인분 Serves 2-3

떡볶이떡 400g
400 grams of tteokbokkitteok

소고기 150g
150 grams of beef

표고버섯 2-3개
2-3 shiitake mushrooms

파프리카 1/2개
1/2 bell pepper

당근 1/4개
1/4 carrot

통깨 1작은술
1 teaspoon sesame seeds

Sauce & Marinade

양념 1 SAUCE 1

간장 1큰술
1 tablespoon soy sauce

참기름 1큰술
1 tablespoon sesame oil

양념 2 SAUCE 2

간장 2큰술
2 tablespoons soy sauce

참기름 1큰술
1 tablespoon sesame oil

설탕 1큰술
1 tablespoon sugar

다진 마늘 1작은술
1 teaspoon crushed garlic

후춧가루 조금
a pinch of ground black pepper

TIPS

* Onion, leek, and other vegetables can also be used. Steep dried shiitakes before using, and feel free to use or omit oyster mushrooms or other varieties of mushroom.

준비 PREPARATION

◆ 떡볶이용 떡은 그대로 사용하고 가래떡은 5cm 정도로 자른 뒤 6등분 한다.
Use tteokbokkitteok as is and if using garaetteok, cut it into 5 cm pieces and divide into 6.

◆ 소고기는 다진 고기를 사용해도 된다.
Minced beef can also be used.

요리 COOKING

1 소고기, 표고버섯, 파프리카, 당근은 얇게 적당한 크기로 썬다.
Cut the beef, shiitake mushrooms, bell peppers, and carrots thinly into appropriately sized pieces.

2 떡은 말랑한 상태로 양념 1을 넣어 버무린다. 딱딱한 떡은 끓는 물에 1분 정도 데친 후 찬물에 헹궈 물기를 빼고 바로 양념 1에 버무린다.
Add sauce 1 to softened tteok and mix. For hard tteok, blanch for about 1 minute in boiling water, then rinse in cold water, drain, and mix into sauce 1.

3 양념 2를 모두 섞어 양념장을 만들고 양념장의 반만 소고기와 표고버섯에 넣어 버무려 재워 둔다.
Mix all the ingredients for sauce 2 to make a marinade, then add half to the beef and shiitake mushrooms, mix, and leave to sit.

4 프라이팬에 양념한 소고기, 표고버섯, 당근을 넣고 2분 정도 볶는다.
Add the marinated beef, shiitake mushrooms, and carrots to a frying pan and stir-fry for 2 minutes.

5 떡과 파프리카, 남은 양념을 넣어 1-2분 정도 더 볶는다.
Add the tteok, bell peppers, and remaining marinade and stir-fry for an additional 1-2 minutes.

6 그릇에 담고 통깨를 뿌린다.
Put in a bowl and sprinkle sesame seeds on top.

Vocabulary

Track 029

재료 INGREDIENTS

간장 [ganjang]
soy sauce

note
This is a basic seasoning used to season Korean food. It is also a typical fermented food, along with doenjang, gochujang, kimchi, etc.

느타리버섯 [neutaribeoseot]
oyster mushroom

note
Along with shiitake mushrooms, oyster mushrooms are the most frequently used type of mushroom in Korean cooking. They are used in stir-fries, stews, seasoned vegetable dishes, etc.

Track 030

요리 COOKING

Base Form	Meaning	Examples
헹구다 [hengguda]	to rinse	• 떡을 찬물에 **헹구고** 물기를 빼세요. Rinse the tteok in cold water and drain the water. • 삶은 당면을 찬물에 **헹구세요**. Rinse the boiled glass noodles in cold water.
버무리다 [beomurida]	to mix	• 떡을 간장과 참기름에 **버무리세요**. Mix the tteok with soy sauce and sesame oil. • **버무려** 놓은 양념을 배추에 넣으세요. Add the mixed marinade to the napa cabbage.
재우다 [jaeuda]	to marinate	• 소고기를 양념에 **재우세요**. Marinate the beef in the sauce. • **재워** 놓은 떡을 프라이팬에 볶으세요. Stir-fry the marinated tteok in a frying pan.

Let's Speak Korean!

짜요? 싱거워요?

Track 031

A 맛이 어때요? 짜요? How's the taste? Is it salty?

B 아니요, 싱거워요. No, it's bland.

짜다 and 싱겁다 are adjectives expressing taste and mean "salty" and "bland," respectively. There are other words expressing taste, such as 맵다, 달다, etc.

Exercise

A 맛이 어때요? How's the taste?

B <u>달아요</u>. It's sweet.

| 짜다 | 싱겁다 | 맵다 |

이건 맵지 않아요.

Track 032

A 궁중떡볶이도 매워요? Is gungjungtteokbokki also spicy?

B 아니요, 이건 맵지 않아요. No, this isn't spicy.

"V/A + −지 않다" is used to negate an action or state. The form is the same regardless of whether there is or isn't a final consonant.

Ex 맵(다) + −지 않다 → 맵지 않아요
달(다) + −지 않다 → 달지 않아요
짜(다) + −지 않다 → 짜지 않아요

Exercise

A <u>달아요</u>? Is it sweet?

| 짜다 | 싱겁다 | 시다 |

B 아니요, <u>달지 않아요</u>. No, it isn't sweet.

| 짜다 | 싱겁다 | 시다 |

비빔밥
Bibimbap

• BIBIMBAP •

Bibimbap is a food that is made by placing different seasoned vegetables and meat on top of rice, adding gochujang or soy sauce, and mixing before eating. In the past, it was called "goldongban" instead of "bibimbap," meaning "to mix dizzily." Bibimbap is a representative Korean food, and is popular with Korean people and of course with foreigners as well. If making the seasoned vegetables is difficult, it can also be mixed and eaten with various stir-fried vegetables and gochujang instead.

재료 INGREDIENTS

2인분 Serves 2

밥 2공기 (400g) 2 bowls
(400 grams) of steamed rice

소고기 150g 150 grams of beef

당근 1/3개 1/3 carrot

애호박 1/3개 1/3 Korean squash

표고버섯 4개
4 shiitake mushrooms

양파 1/2개 1/2 onion

참기름 1큰술
1 tablespoon sesame oil

달걀 2개 2 eggs

소금 약간 a pinch of salt

식용유 2큰술
2 tablespoons cooking oil

Sauce & Marinade

소고기 양념 BEEF MARINADE

간장 1큰술 1 tablespoon soy sauce

설탕 1/2큰술 1/2 tablespoon sugar

다진 마늘 1/2작은술
1/2 teaspoon crushed garlic

참기름 1/2큰술
1/2 tablespoon sesame oil

후춧가루 조금
a pinch of ground black pepper

시금치 나물 SEASONED SPINACH

시금치 150g 150 grams of spinach

간장 2작은술 2 teaspoons soy sauce

참기름 1작은술
1 teaspoon sesame oil

깨소금 약간 a pinch of ground
sesame

비빔 고추장 BIBIM GOCHUJANG

고추장 2큰술
2 tablespoon gochujang

설탕 1/2큰술 1/2 tablespoon sugar

참기름 1큰술
1 tablespoon sesame oil

비빔 간장 BIBIM SOY SAUCE

간장 2큰술 2 tablespoons soy sauce

설탕 1/2큰술 1/2 tablespoon sugar

참기름 1큰술
1 tablespoon sesame oil

준비 PREPARATION

◆ 소고기는 가늘게 썰거나 다진 고기를 이용한다.
Cut beef into thin slices or use ground beef.

◆ 당근, 양파, 표고버섯은 채를 썰고, 호박은 반달썰기 한다. 시금치는 다듬어 씻는다.
Slice the carrots, onions, and shiitake mushrooms, and cut the Korean squash into half-cir-cle slices. Trim and clean the spinach.

◆ 채소 재료는 다른 채소로 대신하거나 빼도 된다.
Vegetables can be substituted with others or omitted.

요리 COOKING

1 소고기에 고기 양념을 모두 넣고 무쳐서 재워 둔다.
Add all the marinade to the beef, season it, and leave it to rest.

2 시금치는 끓는 물에 1~2분 정도 데쳐서 찬물에 헹궈 물기를 꼭 짠다. 그 다음 간장, 참기름, 깨소금을 넣고 무친다.
Blanch the spinach in boiling water for 1-2 minutes, rinse with cold water, and squeeze well. Then season with soy sauce, sesame oil, and ground sesame.

3 당근, 양파, 표고버섯, 호박은 각각 팬에 기름을 두르고 소금을 뿌려 살짝 볶는다.
Coat the pan in oil, then lightly stir-fry the carrots, onions, shiitake mushrooms, and Korean squash separately, sprinkled with salt.

4 재워 둔 소고기는 프라이팬에 볶는다.
Stir-fry the marinated beef in a frying pan.

5 비빔 고추장 또는 비빔 간장 재료를 모두 섞어 양념장을 만들고, 달걀프라이를 만든다.
Mix all the bibim gochujang or bibim soy sauce ingredients to make a sauce, and fry an egg.

6 그릇에 밥을 담고 볶은 채소들과 소고기를 담고 달걀프라이를 올린다. 그 위에 참기름을 넣고 비빔 고추장 또는 비빔 간장을 곁들여 비빈다.
Fill a bowl with steamed rice, add the stir-fried vegetables and beef, and place the fried egg on top. Top with sesame oil, and then garnish with bibim gochujang or bibim soy sauce and mix.

Vocabulary

Track 033

재료 INGREDIENTS

시금치 [sigeumchi]
spinach

note
Spinach, which contains many different vitamins, is eaten seasoned or boiled into soup, and is also used as a minor ingredient in japchae, gimbap, bibimbap, etc.

참기름 [chamgireum]
sesame oil

note
Sesame seeds are roasted and pressed, making the savory aroma strong, so this is used to flavor various foods.

Track 034

요리 COOKING

Base Form	Meaning	Examples
비비다 [bibida]	to mix	• 비빔밥은 밥에 채소를 넣고 **비비세요.** For bibimbap, mix vegetables into rice. • 국수에 간장을 넣고 **비비면** 맛있어요. If you add soy sauce to noodles and mix, it tastes good.
무치다 [muchida]	to season	• 소고기를 양념에 **무쳐서** 재워 두세요. Season the beef with the marinade and leave to sit. • 시금치를 간장과 참기름으로 **무치세요.** Season the spinach with soy sauce and sesame oil.
만들다 [mandeulda]	to make	• 양념장을 **만드세요.** Make the marinade. • 비빔 고추장을 **만들어서** 곁들이세요. Make the bibim gochujang and use as a garnish.

Let's Speak Korean!

⦿ 가끔 먹어요.

A 비빔밥을 자주 먹어요? Do you eat bibimbap often?

B 아니요, 가끔 먹어요. No, I eat it occasionally.

자주(often) and 가끔(occasionally) are adverbs that indicate the degree to which an event or task is repeated. The following words can be used depending on the degree of frequency.

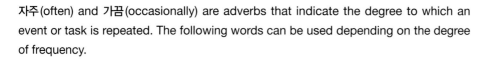

0				100
전혀 안~	거의 안~	가끔	자주	항상 / 언제나
not at all	almost never	occasionally	often	always/any time

Exercise

A 이거 자주 해요? Do you do this often?

B 네, 자주 해요. / 아니요, 가끔 해요. Yes, I often do it. / No, I do it occasionally.

> 항상 / 언제나   전혀 안 / 거의 안

⦿ 비빔밥을 먹어 봤어요?

A 비빔밥을 먹어 봤어요? Have you tried eating bibimbap?

B 네, 비행기에서 먹어 봤어요. Yes, I tried it on a plane.

-아/어 보다 is an expression used to explain that something has been tried or experienced before.

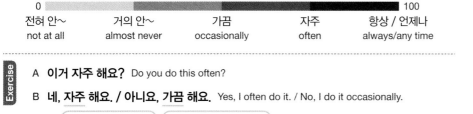

V/A stem with ㅏ/ㅗ + -아 봤어요: 말(다) + -아 봤어요 → 말아 봤어요

V/A stem with other vowels + -어 봤어요: 만들(다) + -어 봤어요 → 만들어 봤어요

하다 → 해 봤어요: 요리하(다) → 요리해 봤어요

Exercise

A 어제 뭐 했어요? What did you do yesterday?

B 김밥을 만들어 봤어요. I tried making gimbap.

> 미역국을 끓이다   해물파전을 부치다

Track 035

Track 036

Be careful!

VOWELS

ㅣ + ㅓ → ㅕ

끓이어 → 끓여
부치어 → 부쳐

김밥
Gimbap

• GIMBAP •

Gimbap is a food made by spreading rice out thin on laver; putting ingredients including pickled radish, egg, and carrots on top; adding ham, eomuk, and various vegetables; and rolling up. Gimbap is easy to eat, so it is famous for being a food for picnics or trips, or in lunchboxes. Depending on the ingredients inside, you can have tuna gimbap, kimchi gimbap, egg gimbap, cheese gimbap, etc., and seeing the colorful combination of the various ingredients adds to the enjoyment.

재료 INGREDIENTS

2-3인분 Serves 2-3

밥 600g
600 grams of steamed rice

단무지 4줄
4 lines of pickled radish

달걀 3개
3 eggs

당근 1/2개
1/2 carrot

햄 100g
100 grams of ham

시금치 200g
200 grams of spinach

참기름 1⅓큰술
1⅓ tablespoons sesame oil

소금 1작은술
1 teaspoon salt

간장 1작은술
1 teaspoon soy sauce

식용유
cooking oil

김밥용 김 4장
4 sheets of laver for gimbap

TIPS

* This is also delicious when braised burdock, cheese, imitation crab meat, tuna, etc. are added.

* Using a roller mat or gimbap mold makes this more convenient.

준비 PREPARATION

◆ 김밥용 단무지는 그대로 사용하고, 통으로 된 단무지는 1cm 정도 두께의 긴 사각 기둥 모양으로 썰어서 사용한다. Use pickled radish made for gimbap as is, or cut whole pickled radish into long, 1 cm thick, rectangular lines.

◆ 염도가 높은 스팸이나 소시지를 햄 대신 사용할 때는 끓는 물에 1~2분 정도 데쳐서 물기를 제거한다. 김은 김밥용 김을 사용해야 찢어지지 않는다. When using spam or sausage with a high salt content instead of ham, blanch in boiling water for 1-2 minutes and then drain. Laver made for gimbap should be used to avoid tearing.

요리 COOKING

1 달걀은 소금을 넣고 풀어 준 후, 프라이팬에 얇게 부쳐서 채를 썰거나 달걀말이처럼 두툼하게 부쳐서 1cm 정도 두께의 긴 사각기둥 형태로 썬다.
Add salt to eggs, beat, and then spread thin and fry in a frying pan and shred, or fry thick like dalgyalmari and cut into rectangular lines 1 cm thick.

2 당근은 채를 썰어 프라이팬에 식용유를 두르고 소금을 뿌려 볶는다.
Shred carrots, coat a frying pan with cooking oil, sprinkle with salt, and stir-fry.

3 햄은 1cm 정도 두께의 긴 사각기둥으로 썰고 프라이팬에 익힌다. 햄이 짧은 경우는 2개를 이어서 사용한다. Cut ham into rectangular lines 1 cm thick and cook in a frying pan. If the ham is short, use two pieces in a row.

4 시금치는 끓는 물에 살짝 삶아 물기를 제거하고 간장과 참기름을 넣고 무친다.
Boil spinach slightly in boiling water, drain, and add soy sauce and sesame oil to season.

5 밥에 소금 1/2작은술, 참기름 1큰술을 넣고 골고루 섞는다.
Add 1/2 teaspoon salt and 1 tablespoon sesame oil to rice and mix evenly.

6 김 위에 밥을 2/3정도 얇고 고르게 펴고, 그 위에 재료를 모두 올리고 눌러 가며 만든다. 김밥을 한입 크기로 썬다.
Spread the rice thinly and evenly over 2/3 of the laver, put the other ingredients on top, and roll while pressing down. Cut the gimbap into bite-sized pieces.

Track 037

재료 INGREDIENTS

단무지 [danmuji]
pickled radish

note
Pickled radish is made by pickling in salt and, after a suitable degree of saltiness has been removed, soaking in a seasoning solution of vinegar, sugar, and gardenia fruits, which are tinged yellow.

김 [gim]
laver

note
Laver is a type of seaweed and is eaten dried, coated with cooking oil, and sprinkled with salt as a side dish, or used dried as is to make gimbap.

Track 038

요리 COOKING

Base Form	Meaning	Examples
부치다 [buchida]	to fry	• 달걀을 얇게 **부치세요**. Fry the eggs spread thin. • 감자전을 **부쳐서** 초간장을 곁들이세요. Fry the gamjajeon and garnish with soy sauce and vinegar mix.
펴다 [pyeoda]	to spread out	• 밥을 고르게 **펴고** 재료를 올리세요. Spread the rice out evenly and put the ingredients on top. • 반죽을 프라이팬에 넣고 둥글게 **펴세요**. Put the batter in a frying pan and spread it out in a circle.
말다 [malda]	to roll up	• 끝에서부터 밥을 **마세요**. Roll up the rice from the end. • 김밥을 **말아서** 소풍을 갑시다. Let's roll up gimbap and go on a picnic.

Let's Speak Korean!

Track 039

🔑 집에서 먹었어요.

A 점심 어디에서 먹었어요? Where did you eat lunch?

B 집에서 먹었어요. I ate at home.

에서 is a postpositional particle that indicates where an action is taking place. It is attached to a place noun in the form of "N + 에서."

Ex 집에서   부엌에서   학교에서   회사에서

Exercise

A 어디에서 만들었어요? Where did you make that?

B 집에서 만들었어요. I made it at home.

식당	부엌	학교	회사

Track 040

🔑 김발로 말아 보세요.

A 김발로 말아 보세요. 더 쉬워요. Try rolling it with a roller mat. It's easier.

B 네, 알겠어요. All right, got it.

–아/어 보세요 is an expression used to recommend that someone try something.

> V/A stem with ㅏ/ㅗ + –아 보세요: 말(다) + –아 보세요 → 말아 봤어요
>
> V/A stem with other vowels + –어 보세요: 만들(다) + –어 보세요 → 만들어 봤어요
>
> 하다 → 해 보세요: 요리하(다) → 요리해 보세요

Exercise

✦ 김밥을 먹어 보세요. Try eating gimbap.

✦ 식혜를 마셔 보세요. Try drinking sikhye.

✦ 시금치를 삶아 보세요. Try boiling the spinach.

Be careful!

VOWEL

ㅏ + ㅓ → ㅕ

마시어 → 마셔

달걀말이

Dalgyalmari

◆ DALGYALMARI ◆

Dalgyalmari is a food made by beating eggs well, adding carrots, green onion, etc., cooking in a pan, and rolling up. It is called “dalgyalmari” or “gyeranmari” (literally “egg rolls”) because it is made by adding beaten eggs to a pan and then rolling. In addition to green onion, carrots, onion, and other chopped vegetables, ham, sausage, cheese, etc. can be applied. It is often used as a side dish in lunchboxes.

재료 INGREDIENTS

2-3인분 Serves 2-3

달걀 5개
5 eggs

당근 15g
15 grams of carrot

대파 20g
20 grams of green onion

소금 1작은술
1 teaspoon salt

설탕 1/3작은술
1/3 teaspoon sugar

식용유 3큰술
3 tablespoons cooking oil

준비 PREPARATION

◆ 달걀은 3개 이상이면 달걀말이의 모양을 만들 수 있으며 달걀이 많아질수록 더 두툼한 달걀말이가 된다.
The shape of the dalgyalmari can be made with an amount of 3 eggs or more, and the more eggs used, the thicker the dalgyalmari.

◆ 채소 대신 치즈를 사용하는 경우는 치즈를 미리 길게 썰어 두었다가 달걀을 말기 시작할 때 넣는다.
If using cheese instead of vegetables, first cut the cheese into long pieces and add when starting to roll up the dalgyalmari.

요리 COOKING

1. 달걀을 볼에 깨뜨려 소금, 설탕을 넣고 젓가락으로 고루 저으며 풀어 준다.
   Break the eggs into a bowl, add salt and sugar, and beat evenly with chopsticks.

2. 대파와 당근은 곱게 다져 달걀을 풀은 물에 넣고 섞는다.
   Finely mince the green onion and carrots, add to the beaten eggs, and mix.

3. 프라이팬을 달군 후 불의 세기를 약불로 줄이고 식용유를 골고루 펴 바른다.
   Heat a frying pan, reduce heat to low, and coat evenly with cooking oil.

4. 프라이팬에 달걀물을 1/3쯤 넣고 얇게 펴고 윗면이 반쯤 익으면 한쪽에서부터 천천히 돌돌 말아 준다.
   Add 1/3 of the egg mixture to the pan, spread out thin, and when the top has cooked halfway, slowly roll up from one edge.

5. 말은 달걀을 한쪽으로 밀고 남은 계란 반죽을 이어서 붓고 다시 말아 준다.
   Push the rolled eggs to one side, pour in remaining egg mixture, and continue to roll.

6. 5의 과정을 달걀 반죽을 다 쓸 때까지 반복하고 달걀말이의 옆면도 잘 익혀 준다. 달걀말이는 잠시 식혀서 적당한 크기로 썬다.
   Repeat step 5 until all the egg mixture is used up and cook the sides of the dalgyalmari well. Cool briefly and cut into appropriately sized pieces.

TIPS

* Onions, mushrooms, bell peppers, etc. can be substituted for green onions and carrots. If you have no vegetables, you can also use eggs alone.

* Well-beaten eggs are called 달걀물 (dalgyalmul).

Vocabulary

Track 041

재료 INGREDIENTS

달걀 [dalgyal]
egg

note

Eggs are used as a main ingredient in Korean food, but are also often used to improve the flavor or shape of a food.

당근 [danggeun]
carrot

note

Carrots are used in japchae, gimbap, and dalgyal-mari, and have an orange color that enhances the color palette of foods.

Track 042

요리 COOKING

Base Form	Meaning	Examples
다지다 [dajida]	to mince	• 채소를 **다져서** 그릇에 넣으세요. Mince the vegetables and put in a bowl. • 대파와 당근은 곱게 **다지세요**. Finely mince the green onion and carrots.
깨뜨리다 [kkaetteurida]	to break	• 달걀을 그릇에 **깨뜨리세요**. Break the eggs into a bowl. • 달걀을 **깨뜨리고** 소금을 넣으세요. Break the eggs and add salt.
풀다 [pulda]	to beat, to whip	• 달걀을 잘 **풀어** 주세요. Beat the eggs well. • 반죽이 뭉치지 않게 **푸세요**. Beat the batter so that it doesn't clump.

Let's Speak Korean!

누가 만들었어요?

Track 043

A 너무 예뻐요. 누가 만들었어요? That's so pretty. Who made it?

B 지수 씨가 만들었어요. Jisoo made it.

누가 is the shortened form of "누구 + 가," 누구 meaning "who" and 가 being a subject marker. "지수 씨," adds 씨(ssi) to a person's name to address that person with respect. When the person being asked the question is answering as the subject, 제가 is used to humble oneself and elevate the other party.

Exercise

A **누가 요리했어요?** Who cooked?

B **엘리스 씨가 했어요.** Alice cooked.

| 제가 | 민수 씨가 | 월터 씨가 |

달걀말이를 만들까요?

Track 044

A 달걀말이를 만들까요? Shall we make dalgyalmari?

B 좋아요. 달걀은 있어요. Great. We have eggs.

"V + -(으)ㄹ까요?" is a sentence final ending used to suggest something to another person.

Final consonant O + -을까요?: 넣(다) + -을까요 → 넣을까요?

Final consonant X + -ㄹ까요?: 빼(다) + -ㄹ까요 → 뺄까요?

Exercise

A **한국 음식을 만들까요?** Shall we make Korean food?

| 먹다 | 요리하다 |

B **네, 좋아요.** Yes, I'd like that.

계란찜
Gyeranjjim

◆ GYERANJJIM ◆

Gyeranjjim (also called dalgyaljjim) is a steamed dish made by beating eggs, mixing in water, and seasoning with salt or salted shrimp.

By adding carrots, onion, green onion, etc. to the beaten eggs, you can make beautifully colored gyeranjjim. Gyeranjjim is soft and the taste is not too strong, so it is a popular side dish for children and also goes well with spicy foods. These days, it is popular to cook it in a ttukbaegi (an earthenware pot) directly over a flame; this is called "poktan gyeranjjim" (a "gyeranjjim bomb").

재료 INGREDIENTS

 2인분 Serves 2

달걀 4개
4 eggs

새우젓 1큰술
(또는 소금 1/2작은술)
1 tablespoon salted shrimp
(or 1/2 teaspoon salt)

설탕 1/3작은술
1/3 teaspoon sugar

물 80ml
80 milliliters of water

대파 20g
20 grams of green onion

준비 PREPARATION

◆ 달걀의 양은 찜 용기와 인원수를 고려하여 가감한다.
  Add or subtract eggs depending on the size of the pot and the number of people.

◆ 대파는 송송 썰고 새우젓은 곱게 다진다.
  Slice the green onion and finely mince the salted shrimp.

요리 COOKING

1️⃣ 그릇에 달걀을 깨뜨리고 새우젓 (또는 소금)과 설탕을 넣고 잘 섞은 후 물을 넣고 다시 잘 섞는다.
  Break eggs in a bowl, add salted shrimp (or salt) and sugar, mix well, add water, and mix again.

2️⃣ 뚝배기에 달걀물을 80% 정도 붓고 중약불로 가열한다.
  Pour the egg mixture to fill 80% of ttukbaegi pot and heat over medium-low heat.

3️⃣ 달걀물이 뚝배기에 눌어붙지 않도록 숟가락으로 바닥을 긁으며 계속 저어 준다.
  Stir continuously scraping the bottom of ttukbaegi pot with a spoon so that the egg mixture does not stick to the pot.

4️⃣ 달걀이 몽글몽글하게 익으면 대파를 넣고 섞는다.
  When the eggs have cooked until lumpy, add the green onion and mix.

5️⃣ 달걀이 80% 정도 익으면 다른 뚝배기 또는 깊이가 있는 그릇으로 뚜껑처럼 덮어 최대한 약불로 줄이고 3~4분쯤 익힌다.
  When the eggs are about 80% cooked, cover using another ttukbaegi pot or a deep bowl as a lid, reduce the heat as low as possible, and cook for 3-4 minutes.

6️⃣ 뚜껑에서 김이 나면 불을 끄고 1분쯤 더 기다렸다가 뚜껑을 열고 대파 3~4조각으로 장식을 하여 마무리한다.
  When steam comes out from the lid, turn off the heat, wait another minute, open the lid, and finish by decorating with 3-4 pieces of green onion.

Tips

* If you don't have salted shrimp, use salt.

* Add water and eggs in a ratio of approximately 1:3.

Track 045

재료 INGREDIENTS

계란 [gyeran]
egg

note
Dalgyal is a native Korean word and gyeran is a Sino-Korean word with the same meaning. Both are commonly used.

새우젓 [saeujeot]
salted shrimp

note
As a type of salted seafood made by pickling shrimp in salt, this is used when making kimchi, when seasoning jjigae or guk, etc. It also goes well with pork.

Track 046

요리 COOKING

Base Form	Meaning	Examples
젓다 [jeot-tta]	to stir	• 달걀물을 넣고 바닥까지 잘 **저으세요**. Add the egg mixture and stir well from the bottom. • 소금을 넣고 **저은** 후 뚝배기에 담으세요. Add salt and, after stirring, put into a ttukbaegi pot.
익히다 [ikida]	to cook	• 뚜껑을 덮고 3–4분 정도 **익히세요**. Cover with a lid and cook for 3-4 minutes. • 윗면이 **익으면** 뒤집으세요. Once the top has cooked, flip it over.
기다리다 [gidarida]	to wait	• 뚜껑을 덮고 **기다려야** 돼요. You should cover it with a lid and wait. • 국물이 우러날 때까지 **기다리세요**. Wait for the broth to steep.

Let's Speak Korean!

Track 047

─○ 기다려야 돼요.

A 지금 뚜껑을 열까요? Shall I open the lid now?

B 아니요, 기다려야 돼요. No, you have to wait.

When –아/어야 돼요 is added to a verb, it indicates the necessity of an action or situation. "V + –아/어야 돼요?" is the interrogative form.

> V stem with ㅏ/ㅗ + –아/어야 돼요: 가(다) + –아야 돼요 → 가야 돼요
>
> V stem with other vowels + –아/어야 돼요: 기다리(다) + –어야 돼요 → 기다려야 돼요
>
> 하다 → 해야 돼요: 공부하다 → 공부해야 돼요

 Exercise

A 영화를 볼까요? Shall we watch a movie?

B 미안해요. 안 돼요. 공부해야 돼요. I'm sorry. I can't. I have to study.

집에 가다	밥을 먹다	일하다

Track 048

─○ 대파를 넣고 섞으세요.

A 이제 뭘 넣을까요? What should I add next?

B 대파를 넣고 섞으세요. Add the green onion and mix.

–고 is a word ending that connects actions in a task in order. In the pattern "V₁ + –고 V₂," V₁ is carried out before V₂.

Ex 넣(다) + –고 젓다 → 넣고 젓다
덮(다) + –고 익히다 → 덮고 익히다

 Exercise

✦ 뚜껑을 덮고 익히세요. Cover with a lid and cook.

✦ 소금을 넣고 저으세요. Add salt and stir.

두부부침
Dububchim

• DUBUBUCHIM •

This is a food made by frying tofu in perilla oil until golden brown, and
is eaten dipped in soy sauce to which sesame oil and ground sesame have
been added. The flavor of the perilla oil and the savory taste of the tofu go
well together. Tofu is an ingredient eaten regularly which has been favored
and enjoyed since ancient times by the common people for protein intake.
Dububuchim is also one of the types of jeon made during the holidays.
Nowadays, mild dububuchim dredged in egg mixture is also made.

고소한 두부부침 MAKING FLAVORFUL DUBUBUCHIM

재료 INGREDIENTS

2인분 Serves 2

두부 1모 (300g)
1 block (300 grams) of tofu

들기름 2큰술
2 tablespoons perilla oil

식용유 1큰술
1 tablespoon cooking oil

소금 1/2작은술
1/2 teaspoon salt

Sauce & Marinade

간장 1큰술
1 tablespoon soy sauce

참기름 1/2큰술
1/2 tablespoon sesame oil

깨소금 1/2작은술
1/2 teaspoon ground sesame

1 두부는 1cm 정도 두께로 썰어 물기를 제거하고 소금으로 밑간을 한다.
Cut the tofu into pieces 1 cm thick, remove moisture, and season with salt.

2 팬을 달구어서 들기름과 식용유를 두르고 중약불로 줄여 두부를 넣는다.
Heat a pan, coat in perilla oil and cooking oil, reduce heat to medium-low, and add tofu.

3 약 2분 정도 지난 후 두부의 아래쪽 면이 노릇하게 구워지면 뒤집고, 반대편도 노릇하게 굽는다. 두부는 잘 부서지기 때문에 한 번만 뒤집는 것이 좋다.
After 2 minutes, when the bottom side of the tofu is pan-fried to golden brown, flip and continue to pan-fry until the other side is also golden brown. Because the tofu breaks easily, it is best to flip only once.

4 간장, 참기름, 깨소금을 섞어 양념장을 곁들인다.
Mix soy sauce, sesame oil, and ground sesame, and serve together with sauce.

부드러운 두부부침 MAKING MILD DUBUBUCHIM

재료 INGREDIENTS

2인분 Serves 2

두부 1모 (300g)
1 block (300 grams) of tofu

달걀 2개
2 eggs

밀가루 3큰술
3 tablespoons flour

소금 1작은술
1 teaspoon salt

식용유 3큰술
3 tablespoons cooking oil

1 두부는 적당한 크기로 썰어 물기를 제거하고 소금으로 밑간을 한다.
Cut the tofu into appropriately sized pieces, remove moisture, and season with salt.

2 달걀에 소금을 넣고 잘 풀어 준다.
Add salt to the eggs and beat well.

3 두부에 밀가루를 고루 묻히고 달걀물에 담갔다가 프라이팬에 지진다.
Coat tofu evenly with flour, dip in egg mixture, and fry in frying pan.

4 중약불에서 구워야 노릇하게 구워지며, 한 면이 노릇해지면 뒤집어서 익힌다.
For a golden-brown fry, medium-low heat should be used, and when one side is golden brown, flip and continue to cook.

Track 049

재료 INGREDIENTS

두부 [dubu]
tofu

note
Tofu is made by soaking soy beans, grinding and boiling them, and then adding salt water to solidify. Because tofu is made only of soy beans, it is a food that is rich in protein.

들기름 [deulgireum]
perilla oil

note
Perilla oil has a unique, flavorful taste and fragrance different to those of sesame oil, so it is used as an ingredient to enhance the flavor of foods.

Track 050

요리 COOKING

Base Form	Meaning	Examples
뒤집다 [dwijiptta]	to turn over, to flip	• 아래쪽이 익으면 두부를 **뒤집으세요**. Once the bottom side has cooked, turn over the tofu. • 두부는 한 번만 **뒤집고** 불을 끄세요. Flip the tofu just once and turn off the heat.
부서지다 [buseojida]	to break	• 두부는 잘 **부서져요**. Tofu breaks easily. • 두부가 **부서지지** 않게 조심하세요. Be careful that the tofu doesn't break.
굽다 [guptta]	to pan-fry, to grill	• 앞뒤로 노릇노릇하게 **구우세요**. Pan-fry the top and bottom to golden brown. • 기름을 두른 팬에 **구우면** 맛있어요. It tastes good if grilled in a pan coated with oil.

Let's Speak Korean!

🔑 뒤집어도 돼요?

Track 051

A 두부를 뒤집어도 돼요? Can I flip the tofu?

B 네, 뒤집어도 돼요. / 아니요, 안 돼요. Yes, you can flip it. / No, don't.

"V + −아/어도 돼요?" is used when asking for another person's permission to do an action. For an affirmative answer, "V + −아/어도 돼요" is used, and for a negative answer, 안 돼요 is used.

> V stem with ㅏ/ㅗ + −아도 돼요: 닫(다) + −아도 돼요 → 닫아도 돼요
>
> V stem with other vowels + −어도 돼요: 뒤집(다) + −어도 돼요 → 뒤집어도 돼요
>
> 하다 → 해도 돼요: 사용하다 → 사용해도 돼요

Exercise

A 이거 먹어도 돼요? Can I eat this?

B 네, 먹어도 돼요. / 아니요, 안 돼요 Yes, you can eat it. / No, don't

🔑 뜨거우니까 조심하세요.

Track 052

A 뜨거우니까 조심하세요. It's hot, so be careful.

B 네, 고마워요. All right, thank you.

"V/A + −(으)니까" is a connective ending used to indicate that the preceding clause is the reason or basis for the following clause.

> Final consonant O + −으니까: 먹(다) + −으니까 → 먹으니까
>
> Final consonant X + −니까: 부서지(다) + −니까 → 부서지니까

Exercise

✦ 밥을 먹으니까 배불러요. I had a meal, so I'm full.

✦ 두부가 부서지니까 천천히 뒤집으세요. Tofu breaks easily, so turn it over slowly.

✦ 김치가 익으니까 맛있어요. The kimchi is ripe, so it's delicious.

두부김치

Dubukimchi

• DUBUKIMCHI •

Dubukimchi is a food made by adding stir-fried kimchi to heated tofu. With
the white tofu and the red kimchi together, just looking at this dish is enough
to whet your appetite, and your mouth will enjoy how the soft, savory tofu
combines with the crispy, deeply flavored kimchi. It is often eaten as a
side dish and also goes well with Korea's typical alcoholic drinks,
soju and makgeolli, making it a popular snack while drinking.

재료 INGREDIENTS

2-3인분 Serves 2-3

두부 1모 (300g)
1 block (300 grams) of tofu

김치 250g
250 grams of kimchi

양파 1/2개
1/2 onion

대파 20g
20 grams of green onion

참기름 1큰술
1 tablespoon sesame oil

고춧가루 1큰술
1 tablespoon red pepper powder

다진 마늘 1/2큰술
1/2 tablespoon crushed garlic

식용유 1큰술
1 tablespoon cooking oil

설탕 1/2큰술
1/2 tablespoon sugar

물 1/2컵
1/2 cup of water

깨소금 1/2큰술
1/2 tablespoon ground sesame

소금 약간
a pinch of salt

◀ TIPS ▶

* Whole sesame seeds can be substituted for ground sesame.

* Sour kimchi should be used for the best taste.

준비 PREPARATION

◆ 신김치는 먹기 좋은 크기로 썬다.
Cut the sour kimchi into pieces a good size for eating.

◆ 대파는 어슷썰기 하고, 양파는 굵게 채 썬다.
Slice the green onion diagonally and shred the onion into thick pieces.

요리 COOKING

1 달군 팬에 식용유를 두른 후 양파를 2분 정도 볶는다.
After coating a heated frying pan with cooking oil, stir-fry the onion for 2 minutes.

2 신김치, 고춧가루, 설탕, 다진 마늘, 물을 넣고 중약불에서 8분 정도 더 볶는다.
Add the sour kimchi, red pepper powder, sugar, crushed garlic, and water, and continue to stir-fry over medium-low heat for 8 minutes.

3 물기가 거의 없어지면 대파와 참기름을 넣고 1분 정도 더 볶고, 깨소금 또는 통깨를 뿌려 완성한다.
Once the water is almost completely gone, add the green onion and sesame oil and stir-fry for another minute, then sprinkle with ground sesame or whole sesame seeds to complete.

4 끓는 물에 소금을 한 꼬집 넣고 두부를 1분 정도 데친다.
Add a pinch of salt to boiling water and blanch tofu for for about 1 minute.

5 데친 두부는 먹기 좋은 크기로 썬다.
Cut the blanched tofu into pieces a good size for eating.

6 접시에 두부를 담고 두부에 닿지 않게 김치를 한쪽에 담는다.
Put the tofu on a plate and put the kimchi to the other side so that it isn't touching the tofu.

Vocabulary

재료 INGREDIENTS

양파 [yangpa]
onion

note

When cooked, onions have a sweet taste. This vegetable is a typical ingredient used in various Korean foods such as stews, meat dishes, stir-fries, etc.

깨소금 [kkaesogeum]
ground sesame

note

Ground sesame is made of stir-fried, crushed, sesame seeds and is sometimes ground with a little added salt. It has a savory taste and smell, and is decorative, so it is used in almost all Korean foods.

요리 COOKING

Base Form	Meaning	Examples
데치다 [dechida]	to blanch	• 두부를 끓는 물에 **데치세요**. Blanch the tofu in boiling water. • 시금치를 **데쳐서** 물기를 제거하세요. Blanch the spinach and remove the water.
뿌리다 [ppurida]	to sprinkle	• 깨소금을 **뿌리세요**. Sprinkle ground sesame. • 후춧가루를 **뿌려서** 재워 두세요. Sprinkle ground black pepper and leave to sit.
먹다 [meoktta]	to eat	• 두부와 김치를 같이 **먹으면** 맛있어요. Tofu and kimchi taste good when eaten together. • 김치를 **먹기** 좋은 크기로 썰어 주세요. Cut the kimchi into pieces a good size for eating.

Let's Speak Korean!

━○ 김치를 볶아 주세요.

A 김치를 어떻게 할까요? What should I do with the kimchi?

B 김치를 볶아 주세요. Please stir-fry the kimchi.

"V + –아/어 주다" expresses that an action is being done for another person. It is mainly used when offering or promising to do something for someone, or when asking someone for help.

> V stem with ㅏ/ㅗ + –아 주세요: 볶(다) + –아 주세요 → 볶아 주세요
>
> V stem with other vowels + –어 주세요: 뿌리(다) + –어 주세요 → 뿌려 주세요
>
> 하다 → 해 주세요: 요리하다 → 요리해 주세요

A 그다음은 뭘 할까요? What should I do next?

B 김치를 볶아 주세요. Please stir-fry the kimchi.

깨소금을 뿌리다	양파를 썰다

━○ 김치가 조금 매워요.

A 김치가 매워요? Is kimchi spicy?

B 네, 김치가 조금 매워요. Yes, kimchi is a little spicy.

When 맵다(spicy) is combined with the ending –어요, which starts with a vowel, the final consonant ㅂ in the verb stem is changed to 우, which is called an "irregular ㅂ." This applies to 굽다, 아름답다, etc.

Ex 맵(다) + –어요 → 매워요   굽(다) + –어요 → 구워요

A 이거 어떻게 해요? How do I make this?

B 프라이팬에 **구워요**. Grill it in a frying pan.

A 이 그림 어때요? How is this drawing?

B 너무 **아름다워요**. It's so beautiful.

순두부찌개

Sundubujjigae

• SUNDUBUJJIGAE •

Sundubujjigae is a food made by adding pork, beef, shellfish, etc. and red pepper powder to soft tofu, and then boiling until bubbling. It is a dish that is full of the harmony of a spicy and refreshing broth that whets your appetite and soft tofu that calms the spice in your mouth. Boiled in a ttukbaegi and topped with an egg, the sight and sound of bubbling sundubujjigae alone will make your mouth water.

재료 INGREDIENTS

2인분 Serves 2

순두부 1팩 (400g)
1 pack (400 grams) of soft tofu

돼지고기 100g
100 grams of pork

양파 1/2개
1/2 onion

대파 20g
20 grams of green onion

고춧가루 1큰술
1 tablespoon red pepper powder

달걀 1개
1 egg

참기름 1큰술
1 tablespoon sesame oil

식용유 1큰술
1 tablespoon cooking oil

국간장 2큰술
2 tablespoons Korean-style soy sauce

다진 마늘 1작은술
1 teaspoon crushed garlic

물 2컵
2 cups of water

--- **TIPS** ---
* This tastes good if short-necked clams are added.

준비 PREPARATION

◆ 돼지고기는 간 것을 사용하고 덩어리일 때는 다지듯이 작게 썬다.
Use ground pork, or if using chunks of pork, cut into small pieces as if mincing.

요리 COOKING

1 대파와 양파는 다지듯이 작게 썬다.
Slice green onion and onion into small pieces as if mincing.

2 냄비에 식용유와 참기름을 넣고 중약불에서 대파, 양파, 돼지고기를 같이 볶는다.
Put cooking oil and sesame oil in a pot, then stir-fry green onion, onion, and pork together over medium-low heat.

3 돼지고기의 기름이 배어 나오면 고춧가루를 넣고 약불에서 1분 정도 더 볶아서 빨간색 고추기름이 생기도록 한다.
When the grease begins to come out of the pork, add red pepper powder and continue to stir-fry over low heat for another minute until red-colored chili oil is formed.

4 고추기름이 나오면 물을 붓고 국간장을 넣어 5분 정도 끓인다. 바지락조개를 추가한다면 이때 넣는다.
Once you have chili oil, pour in the water and add the Korean-style soy sauce, then boil for 5 minutes. If you are going to use short-necked clams, add them now.

5 찌개가 끓어오르면 순두부를 숟가락으로 떠서 넣고, 다진 마늘도 넣는다.
When the soup comes to a boil, add the soft tofu in with a spoon, then add the crushed garlic.

6 찌개가 다시 끓으면 달걀을 넣고 불을 끈다.
Once the soup is boiling again, add an egg to it and turn off the heat.

Track 057

재료 INGREDIENTS

순두부 [sundubu]
soft tofu

note
During the tofu-making process, when the soy milk solidifies, soft tofu is eaten as is, without pressing or hardening. It is eaten with soy sauce or boiled into stews.

대파 [daepa]
green onion

note
Green onion is an herb used in most Korean foods and is effective for strengthening the immune system and managing cholesterol. It is similar to yet different from leek and fennel.

Track 058

요리 COOKING

Base Form	Meaning	Examples
(간을) 맞추다 [matchuda]	to flavor/ season to one's taste	• 간장으로 간을 **맞추고** 2분 더 끓이세요. Flavor to your taste with soy sauce and boil for another 2 minutes. • 소금으로 간을 **맞추세요**. Flavor to your taste with salt.
사용하다 [sayonghada]	to use	• 돼지고기 대신 소고기를 **사용하세요**. Use beef instead of pork. • 바지락을 **사용한다면** 지금 넣으세요. If you're going to use short-necked clams, add them now.
끓어오르다 [kkeureo-oreuda]	to come to a boil	• 찌개가 **끓어오르면** 달걀을 넣으세요. When the soup comes to a boil, add the egg. • 불이 세서 국물이 금방 **끓어올라요**. The heat is high, so the soup will quickly come to a boil.

Let's Speak Korean!

Track 059

 못 먹어 봤어요.

A 순두부찌개 먹어 봤어요? Have you tried sundubujjigae?

B 아니요, 못 먹어 봤어요. No, I haven't tried it.

못 is used to express the negative meaning that an action indicated by a verb cannot be done or that a state has not been achieved. 못 is used before a verb.

Ex **못** 먹어요   **못** 마셔요

A 매운 음식 먹을 수 있어요? Can you eat spicy food?

B 아니요, <u>**못** 먹어요</u>. No, I can't eat it.

A 순두부찌개를 만들 수 있어요? Can you make sundubujjigae?

B 아니요, <u>**못** 만들어요</u>. No, I can't make it.

Track 060

→○ 조개를 사용한다면 지금 넣으세요.

A 조개는 언제 넣어요? When do I add the clams?

B 조개를 사용한다면 지금 넣으세요. If you're going to use clams, add them now.

"V + −ㄴ다면" is used to indicate a condition for an action that is anticipated to occur.

> Final consonant O + −는다면: 먹(다) + −는다면 → <u>먹는다면</u>
>
> Final consonant X + −ㄴ다면: 사용하(다) + −ㄴ다면 → <u>사용한다면</u>

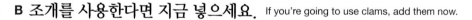

✦ 바지락을 <u>사용한다면</u> 간장과 함께 넣으세요.
  If you're going to use short-necked clams, add them together with soy sauce.

✦ 양파를 <u>넣는다면</u> 돼지고기와 같이 볶으세요.
  If you're going to add onion, stir-fry it together with pork.

✦ 한국 음식을 <u>먹는다면</u> 한국 식당을 알려 줄게요.
  If you're going to eat Korean food, I'll tell you a Korean restaurant.

불고기
Bulgogi

• BULGOGI •

Bulgogi is a food made with thinly sliced beef marinated in soy sauce and other seasonings, and then grilled. The base of bulgogi marinade is pear or sugar, which gives a sweet taste to the soy sauce, and the sweet and salty flavor appeals to everyone. The name "bulgogi" means "grilling meat over a fire," and in the past, marinated meat was placed on a grill and eaten. Nowadays, however, it is common to cook and eat it by stir-frying in a frying pan.

재료 INGREDIENTS

2-3인분 Serves 2-3

소고기 (불고기용) 600g
600 grams of beef (for use in bulgogi)

양파 1개
1 onion

대파 50g
50 grams of green onion

표고버섯 2개
2 shiitake mushrooms

Sauce & Marinade

간장 5큰술
5 tablespoons soy sauce

설탕 2큰술
2 tablespoons sugar

참기름 2큰술
2 tablespoons sesame oil

다진 마늘 1큰술
1 tablespoon crushed garlic

후춧가루 조금
a pinch of ground black pepper

 TIPS

* Other types of mushrooms can be used instead of shiitake mushrooms.

준비 PREPARATION

◆ 소고기는 등심이 좋으며 2mm 두께로 얇게 썰어 준비하며, 질긴 고기는 양파즙이나 배즙에 1시간 정도 재워 두면 연해진다.
Sirloin is a good cut of beef, and can be prepared cut in thin, 2 mm slices. The tough meat becomes tender if left to sit in onion or pear juice for 1 hour.

요리 COOKING

1 소고기는 핏물을 제거하고 한 입 크기로 썬다.
Remove the blood from the beef and cut into bite-sized pieces.

2 양파는 채썰기, 대파는 어슷썰기 하고 표고버섯은 기둥을 제거하고 길게 썬다.
Shred the onion, slice the green onion diagonally, remove the stems from the shiitake mushrooms, and cut into long pieces.

3 그릇에 간장, 설탕, 참기름, 다진 마늘, 후춧가루를 모두 넣고 섞어서 양념장을 만든다.
Mix the soy sauce, sugar, sesame oil, crushed garlic, and ground black pepper all together in a bowl to make the marinade.

4 소고기와 표고버섯에 양념장을 넣고 고루 무쳐서 1시간 정도 재워 둔다.
Add the marinade to the beef and shiitake mushrooms, mix evenly, and leave to marinate for 1 hour.

5 달군 팬에 재워 둔 소고기와 표고버섯, 양파를 넣고 집게나 젓가락으로 잘 풀어 주면서 볶는다.
Put the marinated beef and mushrooms with the onion in a heated pan and stir-fry while using tongs or chopsticks to mix well.

6 고기가 절반쯤 익으면 대파를 넣고 완전히 익혀 마무리한다.
When the meat is about halfway cooked, add the green onion and finish by cooking completely.

Vocabulary

Track 061

재료 INGREDIENTS

소고기 [sogogi]
beef

note
As the preferred meat of Korean people, it can be cooked in soups, steamed, grilled, etc. in almost any recipe.

표고버섯 [pyogobeoseot]
shiitake mushroom

note
Shiitake mushrooms have a rich flavor and a texture similar to meat, so they are often used as ingredients in Korean food. Dried shiitake mushrooms are also often used as an ingredient in stock.

Track 062

요리 COOKING

Base Form	Meaning	Examples
얇다 [yaltta]	to be thin	• 소고기는 **얇게** 썬 것을 준비하세요. Prepare beef cut into thin slices. • 양파 채가 너무 **얇아요**. The onion is cut too thin.
질기다 [jilgida]	to be tough	• 불고기가 너무 **질겨요**. The bulgogi is too tough. • **질긴** 고기는 배즙에 1시간 재워 두세요. Marinate tough meat in pear juice for 1 hour.
연하다 [yeonhada]	to be tender, to be light	• 갈비찜이 너무 맛있고 **연해요**. The galbijjim is so tasty and tender. • 된장을 **연하게** 풀어서 찌개를 끓이세요. Beat the doenjang lightly and boil into stew.

86

Let's Speak Korean!

⟜ 소고기가 있어요?

Track 063

A 소고기가 있어요? Is there any beef?

B 네, 있어요. Yes, there is.

있어요? is a conjugation of 있다 meaning that an object exists, and is used when asking whether or not an object exists. It is usually used in the form of N(이/가) 있어요? and for the affirmative answer, 네, 있어요. is used.

Exercise

A <u>표고버섯이 있어요?</u> Are there any shiitake mushrooms?

양파	김치찌개

B 네, 있어요. Yes, there are.

⟜ 아니요, 없어요.

Track 064

A 대파 있어요? Is there any green onion?

B 아니요, 없어요. No, there isn't.

없어요 is a conjugation of 없다, which has the opposite meaning of 있다. For the negative answer to the question N 있어요?, N 없어요 is used. The conjugations of 있다/없다 are also used when buying objects or when ordering at a restaurant.

Exercise

A 뭐 드시겠어요? What would you like to eat?

B <u>갈비탕 있어요?</u> Is there any galbitang on the menu?

불고기	삼계탕	해물파전

A 아니요, 없어요. / 네, 있어요. No, there isn't. / Yes, there is.

갈비탕
Galbitang

• GALBITANG •

Galbitang is a food made by putting beef ribs in water and boiling for a long
time over low heat so the meat on the ribs is soft and falling off the bone. The
softened meat, which has been boiled for a long time, is eaten off the bones,
which are held, and the dish is most delicious when the deep,
rich broth is soaked up by the white rice and eaten together with kkakdugi.
Beef ribs were and are an expensive ingredient, but a bowl of galbitang is a
food that can fill you up substantially and nourish you.

재료 INGREDIENTS

2-3인분 Serves 2-3

소갈비 1kg
1 kilogram of beef ribs

무 300g
300 grams of radish

양파 1개
1 onion

대파 60g
60 grams of green onion

마늘 5-6개
5-6 cloves of garlic

국간장 2큰술
2 tablespoons Korean-style soy
sauce

소금 약간
a pinch of salt

후춧가루 조금
a pinch of ground black pepper

물 2리터
2 liters of water

다시마 10g
10 grams of kelp

준비 PREPARATION

◆ 갈비는 기름을 떼고 1시간 정도 찬물에 담가 핏물을 뺀다.
Remove the fat from the ribs and soak for 1 hour in cold water to draw out the blood.

요리 COOKING

1 핏물을 뺀 소갈비를 끓는 물에 5분 정도 데친 후 깨끗하게 씻는다.
After blanching the beef ribs, which have been drawn of blood, in boiling water for 5 minutes, wash them until clean.

2 큰 냄비에 크게 자른 무와 양파, 다시마, 마늘, 대파 2/3, 물을 넣고 끓인다.
Add the largely cut radish, the onion, kelp, garlic, 2/3 of the green onion, and water to a large pot and boil.

3 물이 끓으면 갈비를 넣어 1시간 이상 갈비가 연해질 때까지 끓인다.
Once the water boils, add the ribs and continue to boil for at least 1 hour until the ribs are tender.

4 갈비는 건져 내고, 무는 건져서 3×4cm 정도의 크기로 얇게 썬다.
Take out the ribs, then take out the radish and cut into thin 3x4 cm pieces.

5 육수를 면포에 걸러서 간장과 소금으로 간을 맞춘다.
Strain the stock through a cloth, then add soy sauce and salt to season.

6 냄비에 갈비와, 무를 넣고 육수를 부어 5분 정도 끓여서, 그릇에 담아 송송 썬 대파를 얹고 후춧가루를 뿌린다.
Put the ribs and radish in a pot, pour in the stock, and boil for 5 minutes, then put in a bowl, put sliced green onion on top, and sprinkle with ground black pepper.

TIPS
* Kelp can be omitted.

Track 065

재료 INGREDIENTS

소갈비 [sogalbi]
beef ribs

note
Beef ribs are an ingredient in the representative Korean dishes of galbijjim and galbigui, and food made with beef ribs is served on holidays or special days.

무 [mu]
radish

note
As one of the frequently used vegetables in Korean food, radish is a main ingredient alongside napa cabbage in kimchi, and is also used in various ways in seasoned vegetables, soups, braised foods, etc.

Track 066

요리 COOKING

Base Form	Meaning	Examples
빼다 [ppaeda]	to take out, to draw out	• 핏물을 **뺀** 소갈비를 넣어요. Add the beef ribs with the blood drawn out. • 다시마가 없으면 재료에서 **빼세요**. If you don't have kelp, take it out of the ingredients.
떼다 [tteda]	to remove	• 갈비의 기름을 **떼세요**. Remove the grease from the ribs. • 기름을 **떼고** 사용하세요. Remove the fat and use.
씻다 [ssit-tta]	to wash	• 채소를 **씻어서** 물기를 제거하세요. Wash the vegetables and drain the water. • 갈비를 물에 **씻으세요**. Wash the ribs in water.

Let's Speak Korean!

—○ 어디 있어요?

Track 067

A 소금 어디 있어요? Where is the salt?

B 여기 있어요. It's here.

어디, meaning "where," is used in N 어디 있어요? to ask the location or whereabouts of a person or object. You can use 여기/거기/저기 있어요 as an answer, with 여기 indicating a location close to the speaker, 거기 indicating a location near the listener, and 저기 indicating a location far from both.

A **무 어디 있어요?** Where is the radish.

B **여기 있어요.** It's here.

> 거기   저기

—○ 식탁 위에 있어요.

Track 068

A 냄비 어디 있어요? Where is the pot?

B 식탁 위에 있어요. It's on the table.

When you need to explain a specific location in answer to 어디 있어요? you can use the form "위/아래/안/밖 + 에 있어요." 위/아래/안/밖 mean "above," "under," "in," and "out," respectively, and 에 must be attached to them.

A **마늘 샀어요? 어디 있어요?** Did you buy garlic? Where is it?

B **상자 위에 있어요.** It's on top of the box.

> 아래에   안에   밖에

91

갈비구이
Galbigui

◆ GALBIGUI ◆

Galbigui is a food made by spreading out thinly cut beef rib meat, marinating
in a soy-sauce-based marinade, and then grilling over charcoal.
The seasoning is nearly the same as that of bulgogi, but as the cut of beef is
different, there is a difference in the texture and taste. When grilling over
charcoal, the aroma of the charcoal soaks into the meat and adds flavor,
and when grilling in a frying pan, the marinade is soaked up until the
very end, deepening the sweet and salty taste.

재료 INGREDIENTS

2-3인분 Serves 2-3

소갈비 (LA갈비) 1kg
1 kilogram of beef short ribs

간장 5큰술
5 tablespoons soy sauce

설탕 2큰술
2 tablespoons sugar

마늘 3–5개 (10g)
3-5 cloves (10 grams) of garlic

대파 60g
60 grams of green onion

양파 1개
1 onion

참기름 1큰술
1 tablespoon sesame oil

후춧가루 조금
a pinch of ground black pepper

배 1개
1 pear

TIPS

* Pear can be omitted.

준비 PREPARATION

◆ 소갈비는 1cm 정도로 뼈째 가로로 썬 것(LA 갈비)을 준비한다.
Prepare 1 cm thin beef short ribs cut horizontally.

◆ 양파(배 또는 사과)는 강판에 갈거나 믹서기에 갈아서 체에 걸러 즙만 사용한다.
Grate the onion (or pear or apple) with a grater or grind in a blender, then strain and use only the liquid.

요리 COOKING

1️⃣ 갈비는 기름 덩어리를 제거하고 찬물에 30분 정도 담가 핏물을 빼고 깨끗하게 씻는다.
Remove lumps of fat from the ribs, soak in cold water for 30 minutes, draw out the blood, and wash to clean.

2️⃣ 양파즙이나 배즙에 갈비를 20분 이상 재워 둔다.
Let the ribs marinate in onion or pear juice for at least 20 minutes.

3️⃣ 대파와 마늘은 곱게 다진다.
Finely chop the green onion and garlic.

4️⃣ 간장, 설탕, 참기름, 다진 파, 다진 마늘, 후춧가루를 섞어 양념장을 만든다.
Mix soy sauce, sugar, sesame oil, chopped green onion, crushed garlic ground black pepper to make the marinade.

5️⃣ 재워 둔 갈비에 양념장을 골고루 발라 주고 30분 이상 재워 둔다.
Spread the marinade evenly over the ribs and leave to marinate for at least 30 minutes.

6️⃣ 팬에 갈비를 올리고 양념장 1큰술, 물 3큰술 정도를 부어 졸이듯이 굽는다.
Put the ribs in a pan, pour in 1 tablespoon of marinade and 3 tablespoons of water, and grill to boil down.

Vocabulary

재료 INGREDIENTS

LA 갈비 [LA galbi]
beef short ribs

note
Beef short ribs are cut perpendicular to the bone, so the meat is attached to thin sections of bone. Because the rib bones are thin, they are often used in galbigui.

배 [bae]
pear

note
Pears are a refreshing fruit with a sweet taste. As an ingredient in Korean food since long ago, they have been used as a tenderizer in dishes containing beef.

요리 COOKING

Base Form	Meaning	Examples
제거하다 [jegeohada]	to remove	• 국물이 끓을 때 거품을 **제거하세요**. When the broth boils, remove the bubbles. • 뼈에 붙은 기름을 **제거하고** 요리하세요. Remove the fat from the bones and cook.
갈다 [galda]	to grate	• 배를 강판에 **갈아서** 사용해요. Grate and use the pears. • 과일을 믹서기에 **가세요**. Grate the fruit in a blender.
졸이다 [jorida]	to boil down	• 갈비를 **졸이듯이** 구우세요. Grill the ribs so that they boil down. • 국물이 걸쭉할 때까지 **졸이세요**. Boil down the broth until it thickens.

Let's Speak Korean!

Track 071

🔑 갈비구이 만들어요.

A 뭐 만들어요? What are you making?

B 갈비구이 만들어요. I'm making galbigui.

–아/어요 is a sentence ending in informal honorific form that indicates the present tense. It is used when talking to familiar people whom you already know well.

> V/A stem with ㅏ/ㅗ + –아요: 갈(다) + –아요 → 갈<u>아요</u>
>
> V/A stem with other vowels + –어요: 줄이(다) + –어요 → 줄이어요 → 줄<u>여요</u>
>
> 하다 → 해요: 제거하(다) → 제거<u>해요</u>

Exercise

- ✦ 지금 집에 <u>가요</u>. I'm going home now.
- ✦ 마늘을 곱게 <u>다져요</u>. I'm finely mincing the garlic.
- ✦ 고기의 기름을 <u>제거해요</u>. I'm removing the fat from the meat.

Track 072

🔑 점심을 먹어요.

A 뭐 해요? What are you doing?

B 점심을 먹어요. I'm eating lunch.

을/를 is an object marker that indicates that the preceding noun is the object of the sentence.

> Final consonant O + 을: 밥<u>을</u> 　 국<u>을</u>
>
> Final consonant X + 를: 갈비<u>를</u> 　 김치<u>를</u>

Exercise

A 뭐 해요? What are you doing?

B 배를 <u>갈아요</u>. I'm grinding the pear.

| 떡볶이를 먹다 | 육수를 끓이다 | 한국 음식을 요리하다 |

갈비찜
Galbijjim

◆ GALBIJJIM ◆

Galbijjim is a dish made soft by slowly boiling beef or pork ribs with radish,

carrot, shiitake mushrooms, etc. and seasoning with soy sauce.

Ribs, and beef ribs in particular, are the most expensive cut of Korean beef,

and because the meat taken from the cow's ribs has a special taste,

galbijjim can be said to be representative among delicious,

high-quality foods. Accordingly, galbijjim is considered as a food

to be eaten on special days like holidays and birthdays.

재료 INGREDIENTS

2-3인분 Serves 2-3

소갈비 1kg
1 kilogram of beef ribs

대파 10g
10 grams of green onion

무 150g
150 grams of radish

당근 1/2개
1/2 carrot

표고버섯 2-3개
2-3 shiitake mushrooms

물 5컵
5 cups of water

생밤 5-6개
5-6 raw chestnuts

양파 1개
1 onion

배 또는 사과 1개
1 pear or apple

Sauce & Marinade

간장 6큰술
6 tablespoons soy sauce

설탕 2큰술
2 tablespoons sugar

다진 마늘 1큰술
1 tablespoon crushed garlic

다진 대파 1큰술
1 tablespoon minced green onion

참기름 1큰술
1 tablespoon sesame oil

후춧가루 조금
a pinch of ground black pepper

--- TIPS ---

* Chestnuts can be omitted.

* Grate the onion (or pear or apple) with a grater or blender, strain, and use only the liquid.

준비 PREPARATION

◆ 갈비는 찬물에 1시간 이상 담가 핏물을 빼야 되며, 중간에 2-3번 물을 바꾼다. The beef ribs should be soaked in cold water for at least 1 hour to draw out the blood, and the water should be changed 2-3 times during.

◆ 핏물을 뺀 갈비는 끓는 물에 5분 정도 삶은 후 찬물에서 뼈에 붙은 불순물을 깨끗하게 씻어 낸다. After boiling the beef ribs, with blood removed, for 5 minutes in boiling water, and wash clean to remove any leftover matter attahced to the bone.

요리 COOKING

1 양파즙(배즙 또는 사과즙)에 손질한 갈비를 넣고 30분 정도 재워 둔다.
Put the prepared beef ribs in the onion (or pear or apple) juice and marinate for 30 minutes.

2 무와 당근은 한입 크기로 썰고 가장자리를 둥글게 깎는다. 표고버섯은 한입 크기로 썰고 대파는 어슷썰기 한다.
Cut the radish and carrot into bite-sized pieces and cut to round off the edges. Slice the shiitake mushrooms into bite-sized pieces and slice the green onion diagonally.

3 그릇에 양념장 재료를 모두 넣고 잘 섞는다.
Put all the marinade ingredients into a bowl and mix well.

4 냄비에 재워 둔 갈비, 양념장 2/3, 물 5컵을 넣고 센 불에서 끓이다가 국물이 끓으면 중불에서 1시간 정도 끓이면서 위에 뜬 기름을 걷어 낸다.
Put the marinated beef ribs, 2/3 of the marinade, and 5 cups of water in a pot and boil over high heat. When the broth boils, bring to medium heat and continue to boil for one hour, skimming off the oil that floats to the surface.

5 갈비가 연하게 무르면 무, 당근, 버섯, 밤과 남은 양념장을 넣고 20분 정도 더 끓인다. When the beef ribs have softened to tender, add the radish, carrot, mushrooms, chestnuts, and remaining marinade and boil for an additional 20 minutes.

6 어슷썰기 한 대파를 넣고 고루 섞어 불을 끄고 완성한다.
Add the diagonally sliced green onion, mix evenly, turn off the heat, and complete.

Track 073

재료 INGREDIENTS

밤 [bam]
chestnut

note
Chestnuts are used as an additional ingredient in dishes like galbijjim, but are also often eaten raw, roasted, or steamed as a snack.

사과 [sagwa]
apple

note
Apples are eaten as is, but are also used in meat dishes instead of pear in order to tenderize the meat.

Track 074

요리 COOKING

Base Form	Meaning	Examples
삶다 [samtta]	to boil	• 냄비에 물을 붓고 콩을 **삶으세요**. Pour water in the pot and boil the beans. • 갈비를 **삶아서** 찬물에 씻어요. Boil the ribs and wash with cold water.
깎다 [kkaktta]	to cut, to peel	• 당근을 둥글게 **깎으세요**. Cut the carrots round. • 사과를 **깎아 주세요**. Peel the apple.
거두다 [geoduda]	to gather up, to skim off	• 국물을 끓이면서 기름을 **거두세요**. Gather up the oil as you boil the broth. • 거품을 **거두고** 약불에서 끓이세요. Skim off the bubbles and boil over low heat.

Let's Speak Korean!

불을 줄이세요.

A 국물이 끓어요. The broth is boiling.

B 그럼, 불을 줄이세요. Then reduce the heat.

–(으)세요 is attached after a verb stem and can be used when asking another person to perform an action or when giving instructions.

Final consonant O + –으세요: 깎(다) + –으세요 → 깎<u>으세요</u>

Final consonant X + –세요: 줄이(다) + –세요 → 줄이<u>세요</u>

Exercise

✦ 갈비를 <u>삶으세요</u>. Boil the ribs.

✦ 대파를 <u>다지세요</u>. Mince the green onion.

✦ 기름을 <u>걷으세요</u>. Gather up the oil.

얼마나 넣어요?

A 물을 얼마나 넣어요? How much water do I add?

B 다섯 컵 넣<u>으세요</u>. Add 5 cups.

얼마 is a word used in an interrogative sentence to ask about the amount or degree of something. The 나 in 얼마나 plays the role of emphasizing or adding on to the meaning. The 컵 in 다섯 컵 is a word indicating a unit of measurement, and is used as "number + unit noun."

Exercise

A 마늘을 <u>얼마나</u> 넣어요? How much garlic do I add?

B <u>다섯 개</u> 넣으세요. Add five cloves.

A <u>얼마나 삶아요</u>? How much do I boil this?

B <u>5분 삶으세요</u>. Boil it for 5 minutes.

장조림
Jangjorim

• JANGJORIM •

Jangjorim is a side dish made with beef (or pork) cut into large pieces
and braised with soy sauce and sugar. The large pieces of meat are
torn into smaller pieces along the grain and served with soy sauce
as a side dish. As the meat stock, soy sauce, and sugar create a
harmonious savory taste as they cook, you will find your bowl of
rice emptied in an instant.

재료 INGREDIENTS

2-3인분 Serves 2-3

소고기 300g
300 grams of beef

양파 1/2개
1/2 onion

마늘 10개
10 cloves of garlic

간장 6큰술
6 tablespoons soy sauce

설탕 1/2큰술
1/2 tablespoon sugar

물 5컵 (1리터)
5 cups of water (1 liter of water)

표고버섯 2개
2 shiitake mushrooms

대파 1/2대
1/2 green onion

월계수잎 3-4장
3-4 bay leaves

준비 PREPARATION

◆ 소고기는 양지나 사태, 홍두깨살을 사용하는 것이 좋으며, 기름이 적은 부위로 준비한다.
Prepare a cut of beef with little fat; brisket, shank, and eye of round are all good choices.

◆ 고기의 잡냄새를 없애기 위해 고기를 삶을 때 통후추, 생강 등을 사용할 수 있다.
To remove the meat smell from the beef, use whole peppercorns, ginger, etc. while boiling.

요리 COOKING

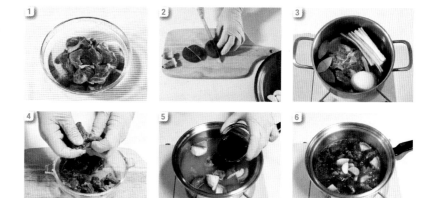

1 소고기는 찬물에 1시간 정도 담가 핏물을 빼고 깨끗이 씻는다.
Soak the beef in cold water for 1 hour, draw out the blood, and wash clean.

2 표고버섯은 기둥을 떼고 2등분 또는 4등분하고 마늘은 그대로 또는 반만 자른다.
Remove the stems from the shiitake mushrooms, divide in halves or quarters, and use cloves of garlic whole or cut into halves.

3 냄비에 물 5컵, 소고기, 대파, 양파, 월계수잎을 넣고 중약불에서 거품을 제거하며 30분 정도 끓인다.
Put 5 cups of water, beef, green onion, onion, and bay leaves in a pot and boil over medium-low heat for 30 minutes, removing the bubbles as you go.

4 육수는 체에 거르고, 고기는 식혀서 먹기 좋은 크기로 결대로 찢거나 자른다.
Strain the stock, cool the meat, and tear or cut along the grain into pieces a good size for eating.

5 냄비에 육수 0.5리터, 소고기, 표고버섯, 간장, 설탕을 넣고 15분 정도 끓인다.
Put 0.5 liters of stock, beef, shiitake mushrooms, soy sauce, and sugar in a pot and boil for 15 minutes.

6 마지막으로 마늘을 넣고 15분 정도 더 끓여 완성한다.
Finally, add the garlic and complete by boiling for an additional 15 minutes.

Vocabulary

Track 077

재료 INGREDIENTS

홍두깨살 [hongdukkaessal]
eye of round

note
As eye of round has nearly no fat, It is an ingredient used when cooking foods with torn meat, such as jangjorim, yukgaejang, and yukpo.

육수 [yukssu]
stock

note
Korean food features many soup dishes using stock, and depending on the ingredients used, there are meat stocks, anchovy stocks, vegetable stocks, etc.

Track 078

요리 COOKING

Base Form	Meaning	Examples
적다 [jeoktta]	to be little, to be small	• 간장의 양이 조금 **적어요**. The amount of soy sauce is a bit small. • 지방이 **적은** 고기를 준비하세요. Prepare meat with little fat.
차다 [chada]	to be cold	• 음식이 식어서 너무 **차요**. The food has cooled off and is too cold. • **찬** 육수를 사용하세요. Use cold stock.
좋다 [jota]	to be good	• 음식은 **좋은** 재료를 사용해야 돼요. Food should be made with good ingredients. • 월계수잎을 사용하면 **좋아요**. It's good if you use bay leaves.

Let's Speak Korean!

—○ 마늘요.

A 뭐가 필요해요? What do you need?

B 마늘요. Garlic.

"N + 요" is used when simply answering a question. 마늘요 shortens and expresses 마늘이 필요해요 as just its core elements.

A 뭐가 필요해요? What do you need?

B <u>간장</u>요. Soy sauce.

설탕	대파

A 어디 가요? Where are you going?

B <u>시장</u>요. To the market.

학교	은행

Track 079

—○ 몇 개 필요해요?

A 몇 개 필요해요? How many do you need?

B 다섯 개 필요해요. I need 5.

몇, meaning "how many," is used when asking a quantity. 개 is a unit of measure for counting objects. Accordingly, you can use the expression 몇 개~? when asking about the number of items.

Ex 몇 개 필요해요? / 있어요? / 넣어요?

5	6	7	8	9	10	+ 개
다섯	여섯	일곱	여덟	아홉	열	

* When 하나/둘/셋/넷 come before 개, they change to 한/두/세/네, respectively.

A 표고버섯이 몇 개 있어요? How many shiitake mushrooms are there?

B 네 개요. (= 네 개 있어요.) Four. (= There are four.)

두 개	다섯 개	열 개

Track 080

소고기뭇국
Sogogi-mutguk

• SOGOGI-MUTGUK •

Sogogi-mutguk is cooked by making broth from beef,

adding radish, and boiling. It can be eaten year-round,

but as radish has a sweet taste in the winter, sogogi-mutguk

eaten in the winter has a deeper, savory flavor. The taste is not too strong,

so it can be consumed by children too, and is a soup eaten by

Korean people in their everyday lives.

재료 INGREDIENTS

2-3인분 Serves 2-3

소고기 (양지머리) 200g
200 grams of beef brisket

무 200g
200 grams of radish

물 6컵
6 cups of water

국간장 2큰술
2 tablespoons Korean-style soy sauce

대파 20g
20 grams of green onion

참기름 1큰술
1 tablespoon sesame oil

다진 마늘 1/2큰술
1/2 tablespoon crushed garlic

소금 1/2작은술
1/2 teaspoon salt

후춧가루 조금
a pinch of ground black pepper

준비 PREPARATION

◆ 소고기는 양지머리를 사용하는 것이 국물 맛이 더욱 좋지만, 다른 부위를 사용해도 된다.
Using beef brisket will give the broth a better taste, but other cuts of meat can also be used.

요리 COOKING

1 소고기는 먹기 좋은 크기로 썬다.
Cut the beef into pieces a good size for eating.

2 무는 3×3cm 정도의 크기로 나박썰기 하고 대파는 어슷썰기 한다.
Cut the radish into thin rectangles of 3×3 cm and slice the green onion diagonally.

3 냄비에 참기름을 두르고 소고기를 넣어 중불에서 2–3분 정도 볶는다.
Coat a pot in sesame oil, add the beef, and stir-fry for 2-3 minutes over medium heat.

4 **3**에 물 6컵을 붓고, 국간장과 무를 넣어 한소끔 끓어 오르면 중약불로 줄이고 20분 정도 무가 익을 때까지 끓인다.
Pour 6 cups of water into step 3, add Korean-style soy sauce and radish, and bring to a boil. Once boiling, reduce heat to medium-low and continue to boil for another 20 minutes until the radish is cooked.

5 무가 익으면 대파와 다진 마늘을 넣고 소금으로 간을 맞추어 5분 정도 더 끓인다.
When the radish is cooked, add the green onion and crushed garlic, flavor with salt to taste, and boil for another 5 minutes.

6 불을 끄고 소고기뭇국 그릇에 담고 후춧가루를 넣어 마무리한다.
Turn off the heat, put the sogogi-mutguk in a bowl, add ground black pepper, and finish.

TIPS

* Because brisket takes longer than other cuts of meat to infuse with the soup, it should be boiled for 5-10 minutes longer in step 4.

Track 081

재료 INGREDIENTS

국간장 [guk-kkanjang]
Korean-style soy sauce

note

Korean-style soy sauce is made by pouring salt water over a block of fermented soy beans and soaking, and is also called "traditional soy sauce" or "Joseon soy sauce." It is used to flavor stews or soups.

양지머리 [yangjimeori]
beef brisket

note

Beef brisket has little fat and is tough, but is often used to make stock because it has the strong flavor of meat protein.

요리 COOKING

Track 082

Base Form	Meaning	Examples
붓다 [but-tta]	to pour	• 소고기를 볶다가 물을 **부으세요**. Stir-fry the beef and then pour in the water. • 육수를 **붓고** 양념을 넣으세요. Pour the stock and add the marinade.
우러나다 [ureonada]	to infuse	• 오래 끓여야 고소한 맛이 **우러나요**. It should boil for a long time to infuse it with a savory taste. • 깊은 맛이 **우러나서** 더 맛있어요. It tastes more delicious because it's infused with a deep flavor.
걸리다 [geollida]	to take (time)	• 이건 시간이 오래 **걸리는** 음식이에요. This is a food that takes a long time to make. • 국물을 끓이는 데 30분쯤 **걸려요**. It takes about 30 minutes to boil soup.

Let's Speak Korean!

Track 083

🔘 안 매워요.

A 이 음식 매워요? Is this food spicy?

B 아니요, 안 매워요. No, it's not spicy.

안 is a negative adverb used to indicate a negative meaning, and is used before verbs and adjectives.

Ex Adjective: 안 매워요   안 예뻐요.

Verb: 안 만들어요.   안 넣어요.

Exercise

A 끓어요? Is it boiling?

B 아니요, 안 끓어요. No, it's not boiling.

A 볶아요? Does it need to be stir-fried?

B 아니요, 안 볶아요. No, it doesn't.

Track 084

🔘 국물만 더 주세요.

A 더 드릴까요? Shall I give you some more?

B 네, 국물만 더 주세요. Yes, please give me some more soup only.

만 is attached after a noun and is used when indicating a limit. It can be expressed as "only" or "just." 더, with the meaning of "more," means that something exceeds a standard.

Ex 사과만   김치만   철수 씨만

Exercise

A 한국 음식 좋아해요? Do you like Korean food?

B 저는 김치만 좋아해요. I only like kimchi.

| 잡채 | 김치찌개 | 닭갈비 |

고추장불고기
Gochujangbulgogi

◆ GOCHUJANGBULGOGI ◆

A grilled food made by cutting pork into thin slices and marinating in
seasoning such as gochujang. Gochujang removes the unique smell from the
pork, and blends together with the fat that comes out of the pork
while stir-frying to soften the meat. If you stir-fry the marinated meat over
medium heat, the gochujang marinade is not too strong and has a charming,
spicy flavor that draws you in.

재료 INGREDIENTS

2-3인분 Serves 2-3

돼지고기 400g
400 grams of pork

양파 1/2개
1/2 onion

대파 50g
50 grams of green onion

풋고추 1개
1 green chili pepper

마늘 3개
3 cloves of garlic

식용유 1큰술
1 tablespoon cooking oil

Sauce & Marinade

고추장 1큰술
1 tablespoon gochujang

간장 1큰술
1 tablespoon soy sauce

고춧가루 1큰술
1 tablespoon red pepper powder

설탕 1큰술
1 tablespoon sugar

다진 마늘 1큰술
1 tablespoon crushed garlic

참기름 1/2큰술
1/2 tablespoon sesame oil

후춧가루 조금
a pinch of ground black pepper

준비 PREPARATION

◆ 돼지고기는 목살이나 삼겹살이 좋으며 불고기용으로 얇게 썬 것을 준비하여 적당한 크기로 썬다.
Pork shoulder or belly is good to use. Prepare by slicing thin for bulgogi and cutting into appropriately sized pieces.

요리 COOKING

1️⃣ 양파는 채썰기 하고, 풋고추는 어슷썰기, 마늘은 편 썰기 한다. 대파는 반으로 나누어 반은 어슷썰기하고, 반은 다지기 한다.
Shred the onion, cut the green chili pepper diagonally, and thinly slice the garlic. Divide the green onion in half, slice one half diagonally, and mince the other half.

2️⃣ 큰 그릇에 양념장 재료를 모두 넣고 양념장을 만든다.
Add all the marinade ingredients to a big bowl and make the marinade.

3️⃣ 양념장에 돼지고기와 양파를 넣고 섞어서 20분 정도 재워 둔다.
Add the pork and onion to the marinade, mix, and leave to marinate for 20 minutes.

4️⃣ 팬에 기름을 두르고 중약불에서 다진 파와 편 썰기 한 마늘을 넣어 볶는다.
Coat a pan with oil, and over medium-low heat, add the minced green onion and sliced garlic and stir-fry.

5️⃣ 파와 마늘이 노릇하게 익으면 재워 둔 돼지고기, 양파와 풋고추를 넣고 중불에서 볶는다.
When the green onion and garlic are cooked to golden brown, add the marinated pork, onion, and green chili pepper and stir-fry over medium heat.

6️⃣ 돼지고기가 익으면 대파를 넣고 센 불에서 1분 정도 더 볶아 완성한다.
When the pork is cooked, add the green onion and stir-fry for another minute over high heat to complete.

Track 085

재료 INGREDIENTS

삼겹살 [sapgyeopssal]
pork belly

note

Pork belly is a cut of meat with alternating lean meat and fat, and because it has a lot of fat, it has a savory taste. In Korean food, it is eaten grilled, stir-fried, or as pyeonyuk (boiled pork slices), but is grilled especially often.

고추장 [gochujang]
gochujang (red chili paste)

note

Gochujang is a unique fermented Korean food, like soy sauce or doenjang. Because it contains red pepper powder, it is one of several spicy seasonings.

Track 086

요리 COOKING

Base Form	Meaning	Examples
적당하다 [jeokdanghada]	to be appropriate	• 삼겹살은 구워 먹기에 **적당해요**. Pork belly is appropriate for grilling. • 돼지고기를 **적당한** 크기로 써세요. Cut the pork into appropriately sized pieces.
크다 [keuda]	to be big	• 사과보다 배가 더 **커요**. Pears are bigger than apples. • 양념장을 **큰** 그릇에 담으세요. Put the marinade in a big bowl.
노릇하다 [noreutada]	to be yellowish, to be golden brown	• 파를 볶았더니 **노릇해졌어요**. The green onion was stir-fried so it turned golden brown. • 두부를 **노릇하게** 지지세요. Fry the tofu to golden brown.

Let's Speak Korean!

Track 087

🔊 고추장불고기 어때요?

A 고추장불고기 어때요? How is the gochujangbulgogi?

B 네, 좋아요. It's good.

어때요? is used when suggesting something to another person or asking for another party's thoughts. The particle after the noun is usually omitted, so it is used in the form of N 어때요?

Ex 김밥 어때요? 볶음밥 어때요?

Exercise

A 뭐 먹을까요? What shall we eat?	**A** 어디 갈까요? Where shall we go?
B 갈비탕 어때요? How about galbitang?	**B** 제주도 어때요? How about Jeju Island?

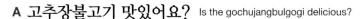

해물파전   한식   놀이공원   바다

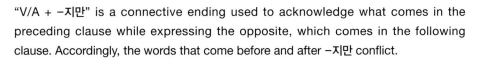

🔊 맵지만 맛있어요.

Track 088

A 고추장불고기 맛있어요? Is the gochujangbulgogi delicious?

B 조금 맵지만 맛있어요. It's a little spicy, but delicious.

"V/A + −지만" is a connective ending used to acknowledge what comes in the preceding clause while expressing the opposite, which comes in the following clause. Accordingly, the words that come before and after −지만 conflict.

Ex 맵(다) + −지만 → 맵지만
크(다) + −지만 → 크지만

Exercise

A 그 사과 맛있어요? Is that apple delicious?

B 크지만 맛없어요. It's big, but isn't delicious.

작다 / 맛있다

111

동그랑땡

Donggeurangttaeng

• DONGGEURANGTTAENG •

Donggeurangttaeng is a type of jeon made by mixing minced pork or beef with tofu and minced vegetables, making it into a round and flat shape, dredging in egg mixture, and frying. Because of its shape, it is also called yukwonjeon (round meat pancakes) or wanjajeon (round pancakes). Donggeurangttaeng eaten hot is full of juice, goes well with vegetables and tofu, and is not greasy. While usually eaten as a side dish or a snack with alcohol, it is a type of jeon frequently made on holidays or birthdays.

112

재료 INGREDIENTS

3인분 Serves 3

돼지고기 400g
400 grams of pork

두부 100g
100 grams of tofu

양파 1/2개
1/2 onion

당근 1/3개
1/3 carrot

대파 30g
30 grams of green onion

달걀 2개
2 eggs

풋고추 1개 또는 홍고추 1개
1 green chili pepper or red chili
pepper

다진 마늘 1/2큰술
1/2 tablespoon crushed garlic

간장 1큰술
1 tablespoon soy sauce

소금 1작은술
1 teaspoon salt

밀가루 2큰술
2 tablespoons flour

후춧가루 조금
a pinch of ground black pepper

식용유 적당량
a good amount of cooking oil

· Tips ·

* Green chili pepper or
red chili pepper can be
omitted.

준비 PREPARATION

◆ 돼지고기는 지방이 적은 부위를 선택하여 다져서 준비한다. 믹서기로 고기를 갈아
서 사용해도 된다.
Choose a cut of pork with little fat and prepare by mincing. You can also grind the meat in
a blender.

◆ 돼지고기 대신 소고기를 사용해도 된다.
Beef can be substituted for pork.

요리 COOKING

1 양파, 당근, 대파, 풋고추 (또는 홍고추)는 작게 다진다.
Finely mince the onion, carrot, green onion, and green chili pepper (or red chili pepper).

2 두부는 면포 등을 사용하여 물기를 제거하고 칼등으로 으깬다.
Use cloth, etc. to remove the water from the tofu, and crush with the back of a knife.

3 볼에 돼지고기, 두부, 다진 채소, 간장, 소금, 다진 마늘, 후춧가루를 넣고 뭉쳐질 때
까지 골고루 섞는다.
Put the pork, tofu, minced vegetables, soy sauce, salt, crushed garlic, and ground black
pepper in a bowl and mix evenly until it lumps together.

4 **3**의 반죽을 지름 4cm, 두께 0.5cm 정도로 둥글고 납작하게 모양을 빚는다.
Shape the mixture from step 3 into a round and flat shape 4 cm in diameter and 0.5 cm thick.

5 달걀에 소금을 넣고 풀어 놓고, 빚어 놓은 동그랑땡에 밀가루를 골고루 묻힌다.
Add salt to the eggs and beat, and coat the shaped donggeurangttaeng evenly with flour.

6 팬에 식용유를 두르고 동그랑땡에 달걀물을 입혀 중약불에서 노릇노릇하게
지진다.
Coat a pan with cooking oil, dredge the donggeurangttaeng in the egg mixture, and fry to
golden brown over medium-low heat.

Vocabulary

Track 089

재료 INGREDIENTS

돼지고기 [dwaejigogi]
pork

note
Pork has a lot of fat, but compared to beef, the price is cheap, and it once served as a source of nutrients for the common people. It is used grilled, for pyeonyuk, in gochujangbulgogi, etc.

홍고추 [hong-gochu]
red chili pepper

note
Dried, well-ripened red peppers are used to add a spicy flavor to steamed dishes, stir-fries, etc. They are also ground into red pepper powder, a common ingredient in Korean cooking.

Track 090

요리 COOKING

Base Form	Meaning	Examples
으깨다 [eukkaeda]	to mash	• 두부를 곱게 **으깨세요.** Finely mash the tofu. • 두부를 **으깨서** 넣으세요. Mash and add the tofu.
빚다 [bit-tta]	to shape	• 둥글납작하게 모양을 **빚으세요.** Shape them round and flat. • 송편을 **빚어서** 찜통에 찌세요. Shape the songpyeon and steam in a steamer.
둥글다 [dunggeulda]	to be round	• **둥근** 접시에 담아 주세요. Put it on a round plate. • 반죽을 **둥글게** 만드세요. Make the dough round.

Let's Speak Korean!

🔘 동그랗게 만들어요.

Track 091

A 어떻게 만들어요? How should I make this?

B 동그랗게 만들어요. Make it round.

–게 is used after an adjective stem, and "A + –게" modifies the verb that follows.

Ex 동그랗(다) + –게 → 동그랗게
예쁘(다) + –게 → 예쁘게

A 어떻게 만들어요? How should I make this?

B 길게 만들어요. Make it long.

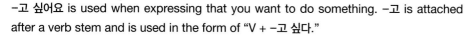

| 작다 | 크다 |

🔘 불고기를 먹고 싶어요.

Track 092

A 뭐 먹고 싶어요? What do you want to eat?

B 불고기를 먹고 싶어요. I want to eat bulgogi.

–고 싶어요 is used when expressing that you want to do something. –고 is attached after a verb stem and is used in the form of "V + –고 싶다."

Ex 먹(다) + –고 싶다 → 먹고 싶다
만들(다) + –고 싶다 → 만들고 싶다

A 뭐 하고 싶어요? What do you want to do?

B 불고기를 만들고 싶어요. I want to make bulgogi.

| 영화를 보다 | 운동을 하다 |

삼계탕
Samgyetang

• SAMGYETANG •

Made by stuffing a young chicken's stomach with glutinous rice, ginger, garlic, and jujubes and boiling, this is a food often eaten to supplement nutrients in the Korean summer, when people sweat a lot and it is easy to become drained. Because it contains nutrients that are good for your body, like protein, it is considered a health food. The ginseng can be left out without a big difference in taste, and to increase the nutrients, abalone can also be added.

재료 INGREDIENTS

2인분 Serves 2

닭 1-2마리 (1.2-1.5kg)
1-2 chickens (1.2-1.5 kilograms)

찹쌀 6큰술
6 tablespoons glutinous rice

마늘 10개
10 cloves of garlic

대추 6개
6 jujubes

인삼 2뿌리
2 ginseng roots

물 1.5리터
1.5 liter of water

대파 20g
20 grams of green onion

소금 1큰술
1 tablespoon salt

후춧가루 조금
a pinch of ground black pepper

준비 PREPARATION

♦ 삼계탕은 600g 정도의 작은 닭을 사용하여 1인분으로 만든다. 따라서 2인분의 경우, 작은 닭 2마리 또는 1.3kg 정도의 닭 1마리를 준비하면 된다.
A small chicken of 600 g makes enough samgyetang for 1 person. Accordingly, if cooking for 2, prepare 2 small chickens or 1 chicken of about 1.3 kg.

요리 COOKING

1 닭은 자르지 말고 통으로 사용하며 꽁지를 자르고 배 속의 지방과 내장을 깨끗하게 제거한다. Don't cut the chicken – use it whole. Cut off the tail and cleanly remove the fat and innards from the chicken's stomach.

2 찹쌀(또는 멥쌀)은 미리 물에 불려 두고, 대파는 송송 썬다. 대추와 마늘, 인삼은 깨끗하게 씻는다. Leave the glutinous (or non-glutinous) rice to soak beforehand and slice the green onion. Wash the jujubes, garlic, and ginseng clean.

3 닭의 배 속에 불린 찹쌀을 먼저 넣고 대추, 마늘, 인삼을 넣고 재료들이 흘러나오지 않도록 꼬치 등을 사용하여 막는다.
First add the soaked glutinous rice to the chicken's stomach, then add the jujubes, garlic, and ginseng, and use skewers, etc. to block the opening so that the ingredients do not spill out.

4 닭의 한쪽 넓적다리 안쪽에 2cm 정도 구멍을 내고, 다른 쪽의 다리를 구멍 안쪽으로 끼워 준다.
Make a 2 cm hole in one of the chicken's thighs and stick the other leg through the hole.

5 큰 냄비에 닭과 물 1.5리터를 넣고 끓이다가 국물이 끓으면 중불에서 1시간 정도 끓인다. Put the chicken and 1.5 liter of water in a large pot and boil, and when the broth has come to a boil, continue to boil over medium heat for an additional hour.

6 닭과 국물을 그릇에 담아 후춧가루를 뿌리고 마무리한다. 소금과 대파는 따로 담는다. Put the chicken and broth in a bowl, sprinkle with ground black pepper, and finish. Put the salt and green onion in separate bowls.

TIPS

* If using ginseng and jujubes is difficult, they can be omitted. If ginseng is not included, this is called "Baeksuk."

* Non-glutinous rice can be used instead of glutinous rice. If there is a hole in the neck of the chicken, put the neck into the hole to block it before adding the glutinous rice to the stomach.

Track 093

재료 INGREDIENTS

인삼 [insam]
ginseng

note
Ginseng, which contains components including saponin, ginsenoside, etc., is known to be nearly entirely toxin-free and effective against all diseases.

찹쌀 [chapssal]
glutinous rice

note
When cooking rice, non-glutinous rice is usually used, but glutinous rice is stickier and better for digestion. Glutinous rice is often used when making tteok, yaksik, etc.

Track 094

요리 COOKING

Base Form	Meaning	Examples
불리다 [bullida]	to soak	• 찹쌀을 미리 **불려** 두세요. Leave the glutinous rice to soak beforehand. • **불린** 표고버섯을 채썰기 하세요. Shred the soaked shiitake mushrooms.
막다 [maktta]	to block (up)	• 닭의 배 속을 **막아요.** Fill the stomach of the chicken. • 찹쌀이 나오지 않도록 **막아야 해요.** It should be blocked so that the glutinous rice does not come out.
마무리하다 [mamurihada]	to finish	• 후춧가루를 뿌리고 **마무리해요.** Sprinkle with ground black pepper and finish. • 채썰기를 **마무리하고** 볶으세요. Finish shredding and stir-fry.

Let's Speak Korean!

Track 095

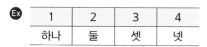

한 마리 필요해요.

A 닭이 몇 마리 필요해요? How many chickens do you need?

B 한 마리 필요해요. I need one.

마리 is a unit of measure used for animals or fish, and is used in the form of "number + 마리." 한 means "one." When combined with a unit of measure, 하나 changes to 한.

Ex

1	2	3	4	→	1	2	3	4	+ 마리
하나	둘	셋	넷		한	두	세	네	

Exercise

A 닭이 몇 마리 있어요? How many chickens are there?

B 한 마리 있어요. (= 한 마리요.) There is one.

세	네	다섯	여섯

Track 096

닭고기지요?

A 이게 닭고기지요? This is chicken, isn't it?

B 네, 닭고기예요. Yes, it's chicken.

(이)지요? is used when confirming an already known fact and is used in the form of "N + (이)지요?" It can also be combined with a verb or adverb stem to express the same meaning.

Final consonant O + 이지요: 찹쌀 + 이지요 → 찹쌀이지요

Final consonant X + 지요: 김치 + 지요 → 김치지요

V/A + −지요: 만들(다) + −지요 → 만들지요   예쁘(다) + −지요 → 예쁘지요

Exercise

A **이게 찹쌀이지요?** This is glutinous rice, isn't it?

대추	삼계탕

B **네, 맞아요.** Yes, that's right.

찜닭
Jjimdak

• JJIMDAK •

Jjimdak is a food made by adding pieces of chicken, potatoes, carrots, and
various other vegetables to a soy sauce marinade, boiling, and then adding
glass noodles. The chicken becomes delicious as it cooks completely while
braising, becoming infused with the broth from the vegetables,
and the glass noodles added at the end go well with the
soy sauce marinade, with a taste like japchae.

재료 INGREDIENTS

2-3인분 Serves 2-3

닭 800g
800 grams of chicken

감자 2개
2 potatoes

당근 1/2개
1/2 carrot

양파 1개
1 onion

대파 40g
40 grams of green onion

청양고추 (풋고추) 2개
2 Cheongyang chili peppers
(green chili peppers)

당면 100g
100 grams of glass noodles

표고버섯 2개
2 shiitake mushrooms

물 3컵
3 cups of water

Sauce & Marinade

간장 6큰술
6 tablespoons soy sauce

설탕 2큰술
2 tablespoons sugar

다진 마늘 2큰술
2 tablespoons crushed garlic

다진 파 2큰술
2 tablespoons chopped green onion

참기름 1큰술
1 tablespoon sesame oil

건고추 1개
1 dried red pepper

Tips

* Shiitake mushrooms can be omitted.

* The dried red pepper can be omitted from the marinade, and dried Thai peppers (prik kee noo) can also be used.

준비 PREPARATION

◆ 닭은 잘라진 것을 준비하고 자르지 않은 닭은 먹기 좋은 크기로 자른다.
Prepare pre-cut chicken or cut uncut chicken into pieces a good size for eating.

요리 COOKING

1 감자, 당근은 1.5cm 두께로, 양파는 2cm 정도로 큼직하게 썬다. 대파와 고추는 어슷썰기 하고, 표고버섯은 한입 크기로 자른다. 당면은 미지근한 물에 30분 정도 불린다.
Cut the potato and carrot to 1.5 cm thick and the onion into large 2 cm pieces. Slice the green onion and peppers diagonally and cut the shiitake mushrooms into bite-sized pieces. Soak the glass noodles in lukewarm water for 30 minutes.

2 잘라서 준비한 닭은 끓는 물에 2분 정도 데친 후 씻는다.
After blanching the cut and prepared chicken in boiling water for 2 minutes, wash it clean.

3 볼에 양념장 재료를 모두 넣고 섞는다. 건고추는 작게 잘라서 넣는다.
Add all the marinade ingredients to a bowl and mix. Cut the dried red pepper into small pieces and add.

4 냄비에 닭과 양념장, 물 3컵을 넣고 국물이 끓으면 중불로 줄여 더 끓인다.
Add the chicken, marinade, and 3 cups of water to a pot and when the broth boils, reduce to medium heat and continue to boil.

5 닭이 반쯤 익으면 감자, 당근, 양파, 표고버섯, 청양고추를 넣고 감자와 닭이 다 익을 때까지 끓인다.
When the chicken is about halfway cooked, add the potatoes, carrots, onion, shiitake mushrooms, and Cheongyang chili pepper and boil until the potatoes and chicken are completely cooked.

6 닭과 감자가 다 익으면 당면과 대파를 넣고 1-2분 더 끓인 후 완성한다.
When the chicken and potatoes have cooked completely, add the glass noodles and green onion, and complete after boiling for another 1-2 minutes.

Track 097

재료 INGREDIENTS

닭고기 [dak-kkogi]
chicken

note
Chicken has less fat and a higher protein content than other kinds of meat. It is used in dishes including samgyetang (a typical summer health food), Korean-style fried chicken, jjimdak, etc.

건고추 [geongochu]
dried red chili pepper

note
Dried red chili pepper is made by drying ripe red chili peppers. It is used to give a more spicy flavor to braised dishes, stir-fries, etc.

Track 098

요리 COOKING

Base Form	Meaning	Examples
들어가다 [deureogada]	to go into, to be used	• 이건 찜닭에 **들어가는** 재료예요. This is an ingredient that goes into jjimdak. • 육수를 만들 때 멸치가 **들어가요**. Anchovies are used when making stock.
큼직하다 [keumjikada]	to be large	• **큼직한** 크기로 썰어 주세요. Cut into large pieces. • 닭이 아주 **큼직해요**. The chicken is very large.
미지근하다 [mijigeunhada]	to be lukewarm	• **미지근한** 물에 불리세요. Soak in lukewarm water. • 미역국이 식어서 **미지근해요**. The miyeokguk has cooled down and is lukewarm.

Let's Speak Korean!

Track 099

무슨 음식 좋아해요?

A 무슨 음식 좋아해요? What kind of food do you like?

B 저는 다 좋아해요. I like everything.

무슨 is used when asking about an object or a thing, and is used in the form of "무슨 + N." To answer "무슨 + N~?" simply, "N + 요" can be used. 다 is an adverb meaning "all" and is used before a verb or adjective.

A <u>무슨 음식 좋아해요</u>? What kind of food do you like?

B <u>김치찌개요.</u> Kimchijjigae.

A <u>무슨 색깔 좋아해요?</u> What color do you like?

B <u>파란색요.</u> Blue.

Track 100

닭고기도 좋아해요?

A 닭고기도 좋아해요? Do you like chicken, too?

B 네, 좋아해요. Yes, I like it.

도 is attached after a noun to express the meaning of "too" or "also," and is used when talking about one thing and then adding in another.

A 무슨 과일 좋아해요? What kind of fruit do you like?

B 사과를 좋아해요. 그리고 <u>딸기도 좋아해요.</u> I like apples. And I also like strawberries.

| 바나나 | 멜론 | 배 |

닭갈비
Dakgalbi

• DAKGALBI •

Dakgalbi is made by marinating boneless chicken legs or chicken cut into pieces in gochujang seasoning, then stir-frying in a pan with cabbage, carrots, and other vegetables. It is also called "Chuncheon dakgalbi" as a bar in Chuncheon first began selling it as grilled marinated chicken instead of grilled pork ribs. It is made by adding tteokbokkitteok, sweet potato, etc. and stir-frying, and also with mozzarella cheese on top. Rice stir-fried in the remaining sauce after eating all the chicken is also delicious.

재료 INGREDIENTS

2인분 Serves 2

닭다리살 500g
500 grams of boneless chicken legs

고구마 또는 감자 1개
1 sweet potato or potato

양파 1/2개
1/2 onion

양배추 100g
100 grams of cabbage

청양고추 (또는 풋고추) 1개
1 Cheongyang chili pepper (or green chili pepper)

대파 30g
30 grams of green onion

식용유 2큰술
2 tablespoons of cooking oil

Sauce & Marinade

고추장 3큰술
3 tablespoons of gochujang

고춧가루 2큰술
2 tablespoons of red pepper powder

간장 2큰술
2 tablespoons soy sauce

설탕 1큰술
1 tablespoon sugar

다진 마늘 1큰술
1 tablespoon crushed garlic

참기름 1큰술
1 tablespoon sesame oil

후춧가루 조금
a pinch of ground black pepper

TIPS

* This is also delicious if, according to your preferences, you add more tteokbokkitteok or top with mozzarella cheese at the end.

준비 PREPARATION

◆ 닭다리살 대신 토막 낸 닭고기를 준비해도 된다.
Chicken cut into pieces can be prepared instead of boneless chicken legs.

요리 COOKING

1 닭다리살은 먹기 좋은 크기로 자른다.
Cut the boneless chicken legs into pieces a good size for eating.

2 볼에 양념장 재료를 넣고 고루 섞은 뒤, 닭다리살을 넣어 30분 정도 재운다.
Put the marinade ingredients in a bowl, and after mixing evenly, add the chicken legs and marinate for 30 minutes.

3 양파는 채를 썰고, 고구마나 감자, 양배추는 한입 크기로 썰고, 청양고추와 대파는 어슷썰기 한다.
Shred the onion, cut the sweet potato or potato and the cabbage into bite-sized pieces, and slice the Cheongyang chili pepper and green onion diagonally.

4 팬을 달구어 식용유를 두르고 닭과 감자 또는 고구마를 먼저 넣고 중불에서 서서히 익힌다.
Heat a pan and coat with cooking oil, add the chicken and potatoes or sweet potatoes first, then slowly cook over medium heat.

5 고구마와 닭이 거의 익으면 양배추와 양파를 넣어 같이 볶는다. 떡볶이떡을 추가하려면 말랑한 상태의 떡을 이때 같이 넣는다.
When the sweet potato and chicken have almost completely cooked, add the cabbage and onion and stir-fry together. If adding tteokbokkitteok, use soft tteok and add them in together at this moment.

6 재료가 모두 익으면 청양고추, 대파를 넣고 1분 정도 더 볶아 완성한다.
When the ingredients have all cooked, add the Cheongyang chili pepper and green onion, and complete by stir-frying for another minute.

Vocabulary

Track 101

재료 INGREDIENTS

양배추 [yangbaechu]
cabbage

note
Cabbage is steamed and used as ssam (vegetable for wraps), and is also used in stir-fry dishes like dakgalbi.

고구마 [goguma]
sweet potato

note
Sweet potatoes are a popular snack in winter, eaten steamed or roasted, and are used as an ingredient in various dishes. The stems of sweet potato shoots are eaten boiled and made into a seasoned vegetable dish.

Track 102

요리 COOKING

Base Form	Meaning	Examples
추가하다 [chugahada]	to add	• 치즈를 **추가하면** 더 맛있어요. It's more delicious if you add cheese. • 간이 부족하면 소금을 **추가하세요**. If the flavor is insufficient, add salt.
말랑하다 [mallanghada]	to be soft	• **말랑한** 떡을 사용하세요. Use soft tteok. • 가래떡을 끓는 물에 데치면 **말랑해요**. If you blanch garaetteok in boiling water, they soften.
완성하다 [wanseonghada]	to complete	• 불을 끄고 **완성하세요**. Turn off the heat and complete. • **완성된** 닭갈비를 그릇에 담으세요. Put the completed dakgalbi in a dish.

Let's Speak Korean!

─○ 고추장하고 고춧가루도 필요해요.

A 고추장 필요해요? Do you need gochujang?

B 네, 고추장하고 고춧가루도 필요해요. Yes, I need gochujang and red pepper powder.

하고 is a postpositional particle used when listing people or objects, and is attached after a noun.

Ex 밥하고 국   설탕하고 간장

A 뭐 드릴까요? What can I get for you?

B 김치볶음밥하고 된장찌개요. Kimchi-bokkeumbap and doenjangjjigae.

양파 / 마늘	소금 / 후춧가루	사과 / 오렌지

─○ 마늘과 참기름도 필요해요.

A 마늘 필요하지요? You need garlic, right?

B 네, 마늘과 참기름도 필요해요. Yes, I need garlic and sesame oil as well.

와/과, like 하고, is a postpositional particle used when listing people or objects, and is attached after a noun.

Final consonant O + 과: 마늘과   호박과   찜닭과
Final consonant X + 와: 사과와   잡채와   오이와

A 뭐 좋아해요? What do you like?

B 김치볶음밥과 된장찌개요. Kimchi-bokkeumbap and doenjangjjigae.

사과 / 오렌지	잡채 / 불고기	호떡 / 떡볶이

127

해물파전

Haemulpajeon

• HAEMULPAJEON •

Pajeon is a type of jeon made by frying scallions dredged in flour batter until golden brown in a frying pan well-coated with oil. In haemulpajeon, which can be considered a type of pajeon, squid, shrimp, and various other kinds of seafood are added on top of the dredged scallions and then fried. Pajeon goes well with makgeolli, and its popularity is increasing along with makgeolli's. The edges are crispy and flavorful, so you can try eating the edges first, and if you make the jeon yourself, you may find your mouth watering as you cook it to a golden brown.

재료 INGREDIENTS

2-3인분 Serves 2-3

쪽파 200g
200 grams of scallions

새우살 100g
100 grams of shrimp

조갯살 100g
100 grams of clams (shelled)

오징어 100g
100 grams of squid

달걀 2개
2 eggs

청양고추 1개
1 Cheongyang chili pepper

식용유 4큰술
4 tablespoons cooking oil

부침 가루 (또는 밀가루) 2컵
2 cups of flour for pan-frying (or wheat flour)

물 2컵
2 cups of water

Sauce & Marinade

초간장
SOY SAUCE AND VINEGAR MIX

간장 2큰술
2 tablespoons soy sauce

식초 1/2큰술
1/2 tablespoon vinegar

TIPS

*If you don't have scallions, you can also use sliced green onion.

준비 PREPARATION

◆ 쪽파는 다듬어 깨끗이 씻고 뿌리 부분이 굵으면 반으로 가른다.
Trim the scallions and wash them clean, and if the roots are thick, cut them in half.

◆ 조갯살과 새우살은 찬물에 헹구어 주고, 오징어는 껍질을 벗겨 길이 0.7×3cm 정도로 작게 자른다. Rinse the clam meat and shrimp in cold water. Peel off the skin of the squid and cut into small strips about 0.7×3 cm.

요리 COOKING

1 쪽파는 프라이팬 크기에 맞춰 2등분하고 청양고추는 어슷썰기 한다.
Divide the scallions in 2 to match the size of the frying pan and slice the Cheongyang chili pepper diagonally.

2 볼에 부침 가루와 물을 넣고 골고루 섞어 반죽한다. 달걀은 잘 풀어 놓는다.
Add the flour for pan-frying and water to a bowl and mix evenly to make a batter. Beat the eggs well.

3 프라이팬을 달구어 중약불로 줄이고 식용유를 넉넉히 두른 후 파를 반죽에 담갔다가 프라이팬에 가지런히 펴서 올린다. 그 위에 새우살, 조갯살, 오징어를 얹고, 반죽을 조금 덮어 준다.
Heat a frying pan and reduce to medium-low heat, coat generously with cooking oil, then dip the scallions in the batter and spread evenly in the frying pan. Put the shrimp, clam meat, and squid on top and cover with a little batter.

4 해물 위에 달걀물을 골고루 끼얹고 청양고추를 올린다.
Pour the beaten eggs evenly over the seafood and add the Cheongyang chili pepper on top.

5 아랫면이 노릇해지면 뒤집고 중약불에서 앞, 뒤를 노릇하게 지진다.
When the bottom becomes golden brown, turn over and fry both the top and bottom over medium-low heat until golden brown.

6 간장과 식초를 섞어 초간장을 만들어 같이 곁들인다.
Mix soy sauce and vinegar to make seasoning soy sauce and vinegar mix and serve together.

Vocabulary

Track 105

재료 INGREDIENTS

조개 [jogae]
clam

note
Because boiling clams in water infuses it with a savory taste, making a clean-tasting and refreshing broth, clams are used as a minor ingredient in various stews, soups, and more, as well as in haemulpajeon, etc.

쪽파 [jjokpa]
scallion

note
Scallions are used often as an herb and are thinner and smaller than green onions, and as they are milder, they are also often used for making pakimchi.

Track 106

요리 COOKING

Base Form	Meaning	Examples
반죽하다 [banjukada]	to knead, to make a batter/dough	• 밀가루와 물을 넣고 **반죽하세요.** Add flour and water to make a batter. • **반죽한** 것을 따뜻한 곳에서 발효시키세요. Let the dough ferment in a warm place.
얹다 [eontta]	to put on (top)	• 반죽 위에 오징어를 **얹으세요.** Put the squid on top of the batter. • 계란찜 위에 파를 **얹고** 완성하세요. Put the green onion on top of the gyeranjjim and complete.
곁들이다 [gyeot-tteurida]	to garnish, to add, to serve with	• 비빔 간장을 **곁들이세요.** Garnish with bibim soy sauce. • 된장국을 **곁들이면** 좋아요. It's good when served with doenjangguk.

Let's Speak Korean!

 Track 107

⊸ 비가 올 때 해물파전을 만들어요.

A 해물파전 좋아해요? Do you like haemulpajeon?

B 네, 좋아해요. 비가 올 때 해물파전을 만들어요.
Yes, I like it. I make haemulpajeon when it rains.

"V + −(으)ㄹ 때" is an expression used to indicate the time when an action or state occurs.

> Final consonant O + −을 때: 끓(다) + −을 때 → 끓을 때
> Final consonant X + −ㄹ 때: 오(다) + −ㄹ 때 → 올 때

A 이건 언제 넣어요? When do I add this?

B 끓을 때 넣으세요. Add that when it boils.

> 반죽하다   볶다   무치다

 Track 108

⊸ 음식을 만드는 중이에요.

A 뭐 해요? What are you doing?

B 음식을 만드는 중이에요. I'm making food.

"V + −는 중이다" is an expression that is used to indicate that the subject of the clause is in the middle of doing something.

Ex 만들(다) + −는 중이에요 → 만드는 중이에요
요리하(다) + −는 중이에요 → 요리하는 중이에요

Be careful!
If 만들다 is followed by a word that starts with ㄴ, then the ㄹ is dropped.
Ex 만들(다) + 는 → 만드는

A 지금 뭐 하는 중이에요? What are you doing right now?

B 해물파전을 만드는 중이에요. I'm making haemulpajeon.

> 요리하다   밀가루를 반죽하다   육수를 끓이다

미역국
Miyeokguk

• MIYEOKGUK •

Miyeokguk is a soup made by soaking dried seaweed and boiling over low heat. Because of the slippery texture of the seaweed, there are people who dislike it, but even they will find it worth trying because they can enjoy the deep taste of the broth. In Korean culture, miyeokguk is a typical food eaten on birthdays, and is known as helping mothers recover after giving birth.

재료 INGREDIENTS

2-3인분 Serves 2-3

마른 미역 20g
20 grams of dried seaweed

소고기 (양지머리) 200g
200 grams of beef brisket

참기름 2큰술
2 tablespoons sesame oil

국간장 2큰술
2 tablespoons Korean-style soy sauce

액젓 1큰술
1 tablespoon fish sauce

다진 마늘 1작은술
1 teaspoon crushed garlic

물 10컵
10 cups of water

준비 PREPARATION

◆ 마른 미역을 찬물에 넣고 30분 정도 불린다.
Put the dried seaweed in cold water and soak for 30 minutes.

◆ 소고기는 찬물에 10분 정도 담가 핏물을 뺀다. 양지머리 대신 다른 부위를 사용할 경우 고기를 납작하고 작게 썬다.
Soak the beef in cold water for 10 minutes and draw out the blood. If using another cut of meat besides brisket, cut into small, flat pieces.

요리 COOKING

1 불린 미역은 깨끗하게 헹궈 먹기 좋게 자른다.
Rinse the soaked seaweed and cut into pieces a good size for eating.

2 냄비에 물 10컵을 넣고 물이 끓으면 소고기를 넣어 중약불로 줄여 40분 정도 끓여 준다.
Add 10 cups of water to a pot and when it boils, add beef and continue to boil over medium-low heat for 40 minutes.

3 소고기가 부드럽게 익으면 고기를 꺼내 손으로 잘게 찢는다.
When the beef has cooked until soft, take it out and tear into small pieces with your hands.

4 냄비에 참기름을 두르고 미역과 찢은 고기, 간장을 넣고 1~2분 정도 볶다가 고기 육수 7컵을 넣고 끓인다.
Coat the pot with sesame oil and add the seaweed, torn meat, and soy sauce and stir-fry for 1-2 minutes, then add 7 cups of the beef stock and boil.

5 국물이 끓으면 중약불로 줄여 20분 정도 끓이다가 액젓으로 간을 맞춘다.
Once the broth is boiling, reduce to medium-low heat and continue boiling for 20 minutes, then season to taste with fish sauce.

6 다진 마늘을 넣고 2분 정도 더 끓여 완성한다.
Add crushed garlic and complete by boiling for an additional 2 minutes.

• TIPS •

*Other cuts of beef can be substituted for brisket.

*If you are using a different cut of beef, coat the pot in sesame oil, add the beef, and stir-fry over medium-low heat, add seaweed and soy sauce, stir-fry for 1-2 minutes, then add 7 cups of water and boil. Complete with step 5-6.

Track 109

재료 INGREDIENTS

미역 [miyeok]
seaweed

note
Seaweed is eaten raw as is, but is more commonly eaten when dried and boiled into soup. In Korea in particular, there is a custom of eating miyeokguk on birthdays.

액젓 [aekjjeot]
fish sauce

note
This is a filtered liquid made by fermenting fish in salt over a long period of time. Depending on the type of fish it is made with, there is anchovy fish sauce, lancefish fish sauce, etc., and is used in soup dishes, kimchi, and more.

Track 110

요리 COOKING

Base Form	Meaning	Examples
깨끗하다 [kkaekkeutada]	to be clean	• 불린 미역을 **깨끗하게** 헹구세요. Rinse the soaked seaweed clean. • 양파를 **깨끗이** 씻으세요. Wash the onions cleanly.
부드럽다 [budeureoptta]	to be soft	• **부드럽게** 익으면 고기를 꺼내세요. When the meat is cooked until soft, remove it. • 계란찜이 너무 **부드러워요.** The gyeranjjim is too soft.
찢다 [jjit-tta]	to tear	• 익은 고기를 **찢으세요.** Tear the cooked meat. • **찢은** 고기를 넣고 볶으세요. Add the torn meat and stir-fry.

Let's Speak Korean!

🔊 10월 5일이에요.

A 생일이 며칠이에요? What date is your birthday?

B 10월 5일이에요. It's October 5th.

며칠 means "date" and is used when asking a date. Korean has 2 number systems, native Korean-based and Sino-Korean, and when reading the date, the Sino-Korean numbers are used, like in this table.

1	2	3	4	5	6	7	8	9	10	O월 O일
일	이	삼	사	오	육	칠	팔	구	십	month day

Track 111

Exercise

A **오늘이 며칠이에요?** What is the date today?

B **12월 1일이에요.** It's December 1st.

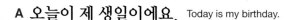
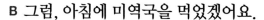

6월 26일   3월 15일

Be careful!
6월 → 유월
10월 → 시월

🔊 미역국을 먹었겠어요.

A 오늘이 제 생일이에요. Today is my birthday.

B 그럼, 아침에 미역국을 먹었겠어요.
Then you must have had miyeokguk this morning.

Track 112

–겠– is a pre-final ending used when expressing a guess about something and is combined with a verb/adjective between the stem and the ending.

Ex 먹(다) + –겠– + –어요 → 먹겠어요 (present)
먹(다) + –었– + –겠– + 다 → 먹었겠어요 (past)

끓(다) + –겠– + –어요 → 끓겠어요 (present)
끓(다) + –었– + –겠– + –어요 → 끓었겠어요 (past)

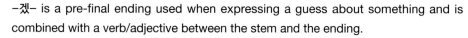

Exercise

✦ **미역국이 정말 맛있<u>겠</u>어요.** The miyeokguk must be very delicious.

✦ **김치가 조금 맵<u>겠</u>어요.** The kimchi seems a little spicy.

새우전
Saeujeon

• SAEUJEON •

Meat, fish, vegetables, etc. that are dredged in flour and egg mixture
and fried in a pan coated in oil are called "jeon" (pancakes).
Saeujeon is another type of jeon. This dish is made using whole shrimp in
their original shape or minced with various vegetables, then dredged
in flour and egg mixture, and fried in a pan. The golden-brown
saeujeon retains a firm texture that makes it enjoyable to chew.
Saeujeon is eaten as a side dish or as a snack with alcohol.

재료 INGREDIENTS

2-3인분 Serves 2-3

새우살 250g
250 grams of shrimp

달걀 2개
2 eggs

밀가루 1/2컵
1/2 cup of flour

소금 1작은술
1 teaspoon salt

후춧가루 조금
a pinch of ground black pepper

식용유 적당량
a good amount of cooking oil

Sauce & Marinade

양념간장 SEASONING SOY SAUCE

간장 1큰술
1 tablespoon soy sauce
식초 1/2큰술
1/2 tablespoon vinegar
통깨 sesame seeds

준비 PREPARATION

◆ 새우는 10cm 정도의 중간 크기 이상이 좋으며, 꼬리 부분만 남기고 껍짓을 벗겨 준비한다.
Shrimp of about 10 cm (medium size or larger) are ideal. Prepare by removing the shell except for the tail.

요리 COOKING

1 새우는 찬물에 헹궈 물기를 제거한다.
Rinse the shrimp in cold water and drain.

2 새우의 등 부분을 반으로 갈라 남은 내장을 제거하고 새우가 구부러지지 않게 앞, 뒤로 살짝 칼집을 낸다.
Cut the shrimp in half along its back and remove any remaining vein, then make small cuts to the front and back so that it does not bend.

3 새우살에 소금과 후춧가루를 뿌려 10분 정도 재워 둔다.
Sprinkle salt and ground black pepper onto the meat of the shrimp and leave to sit for 10 minutes.

4 새우살에 앞, 뒤로 밀가루를 묻히고 달걀에 소금을 넣고 풀어 준다.
Coat the front and back of the shrimp in flour, then add salt to the eggs and beat them.

5 밀가루 묻힌 새우를 달걀물을 입혀 약불에서 뒤집어 가며 익힌다.
Dredge the coated shrimp in the egg mixture and flip while cooking over low heat.

6 간장과 식초, 통깨를 섞어 양념간장을 만들어 같이 곁들인다.
Make seasoning soy sauce by mixing soy sauce, vinegar, and sesame seeds, and serve together.

Track 113

재료 INGREDIENTS

새우 [saeu]
shrimp

note
Large shrimp like jumbo shrimp are roasted or used in stews, etc., while small shrimp are used as a minor ingredient in soups or stews, or to make salted shrimp for use as a seasoning.

후춧가루 [huchukkaru]
ground black pepper

note
The powdered form of black pepper, which was a precious spice up through the Joseon dynasty, is used most often mainly to remove the smell from meat.

Track 114

요리 COOKING

Base Form	Meaning	Examples
준비하다 [junbihada]	to prepare	• 껍질을 깐 새우를 **준비하세요**. Prepare shrimp with the shells removed. • **준비된** 새우를 찬물에 헹구세요. Rinse the prepared shrimp in cold water.
묻히다 [muchida]	to coat	• 새우에 밀가루를 **묻히세요**. Coat the shrimp in flour. • 빵가루를 **묻혀서** 튀기세요. Coat with bread crumbs and deep fry.
입히다 [ipida]	to dredge	• 달걀물을 **입혀서** 익히세요. Dredge in egg mixture then cook. • 동그랑땡에 달걀물을 **입히세요**. Dredge the donggeurangttaeng in egg mixture.

Let's Speak Korean!

🔑 삼백 그램 필요해요.

Track 115

A 새우가 얼마나 필요해요? How much shrimp do you need?

B 삼백 그램 필요해요. I need 300 grams.

When talking about prices and amounts, use the Sino-Korean number system.

1	2	3	4	5	6	7	8	9	10		100	1,000	10,000
일	이	삼	사	오	육	칠	팔	구	십		백	천	만

Exercise

A 설탕이 얼마나 필요해요? How much sugar do you need?

B <u>백오십</u> 그램 필요해요. I need 150 grams.

이백	오십	십칠

🔑 새우전을 먹어 본 적이 있어요?

Track 116

A 새우전을 먹어 본 적이 있어요? Have you eaten saeujeon before?

B 아니요, 없어요. No, I haven't.

–(으)ㄴ 적이 있다 is an expression that combines with a verb and is used to denote a previous experience. The response to this can be a simple, 네, 있어요. ("Yes, I have.") or 아니요, 없어요. ("No, I haven't.")

Exercise

A 삼계탕을 먹어 봤어요? Have you eaten samgyetang before?

B 네, 삼계탕을 먹어 <u>본 적이 있어요</u>. Yes, I've eaten samgyetang before.

A 한국 노래를 <u>들은 적이 있어요</u>? Have you heard a Korean song before?

B 네, 있어요. / 아니요, 없어요. Yes, I have. / No, I haven't.

어묵탕

Eomuktang

• EOMUKTANG •

Eomuk is made by mashing up the meat of fish, adding salt, etc., kneading, and frying. Eomuktang is a food made by taking various types of these eomuk, putting them on skewers, adding plenty of water, and boiling together with radish, onion, anchovies, etc. Piping hot eomuktang comes to mind in the cold winter, and just seeing the broth can warm your body. Along with tteokbokki, kkochi-eomuk (eomuk on skewers) is a typical street food, and with a taste that is not too strong, it is a food that anyone can enjoy.

재료 INGREDIENTS

3-4인분 Serves 3-4

어묵 500g
500 grams of eomuk

표고버섯 2개
2 shiitake mushrooms

대파 60g
60 grams of green onion

양파 1/2개
1/2 onion

무 150g
150 grams of radish

다시마 10g
10 grams of kelp

국물용 멸치 10g
10 grams of anchovies for use in
soup broth

물 6컵
6 cups of water

국간장 2큰술
2 tablespoons Korean-style soy
sauce

후춧가루 조금
a pinch of ground black pepper

나무 꼬치 10개
10 wooden skewers

Sauce & Marinade

양념간장 SEASONING SOY SAUCE

간장 2큰술
2 tablespoons soy sauce

깨소금 또는 연겨자 적당량
a good amount of ground sesame
or light mustard

준비 PREPARATION

◆ 어묵은 보통 얇은 사각 어묵을 많이 사용하지만, 다양한 종류의 어묵을 사용하면 보기에도 화려하고, 여러 가지 맛을 느낄 수 있다.
Thin squares of eomuk are used most often, but if using other kinds of eomuk, the dish looks impressive and you can taste various different flavors.

요리 COOKING

1 무는 큼직하게 썰고, 대파는 4cm 정도로 썬다. 표고버섯은 모양을 낸다.
Cut the radish into fairly large pieces and slice the green onion into 4 cm pieces. Make the mushrooms look shapely.

2 냄비에 물, 양파, 무, 다시마, 멸치를 넣고 끓으면 국간장을 넣고 중약불로 20분 정도 끓인다.
In a pot, add water, onion, radish, kelp, and anchovies, and boil, then add Korean-style soy sauce and continue to boil over medium-low heat for 20 minutes.

3 육수가 끓는 동안 어묵을 접어서 먹기 좋게 꼬치에 끼운다.
While the stock is boiling, fold the eomuk and put it on the skewers to make easy to eat.

4 육수가 만들어지면 무 2-3개와 다시마는 건져 두고, 건더기를 체에 거르세요.
When the stock has been made, remove 2-3 radishes and the kelp, then strain out the solid ingredients.

5 냄비에 꼬치에 끼운 어묵과 건져 놓은 무와 다시마, 대파, 표고버섯을 넣고 어묵이 잠길 정도의 육수를 붓고 10분 정도 끓인다.
In a pot, add the skewered-eomuk, the removed radishes and kelp, green onion, and shiitake mushrooms, pour in enough stock to submerge the eomuk, and boil for 10 minutes.

6 먹기 전에 후춧가루를 뿌리고 양념장을 곁들인다.
Before eating, sprinkle with ground black pepper, and serve with seasoning soy sauce.

Vocabulary

재료 INGREDIENTS

어묵 [eomuk]
eomuk (fish cake)

note
Eomuk is made by adding salt, etc. to minced fish and cooking to solidify. Eomuk exists in different thicknesses and shapes, and is used in eomuktang, stir-fries, etc.

멸치 [myeolchi]
anchovy

note
Anchovies are a typical ingredient in side dishes, and depending on the type, are also used as a typical ingredient in stocks for soup.

요리 COOKING

Base Form	Meaning	Examples
끼우다 [kkiuda]	to put onto	• 어묵을 꼬치에 **끼우세요**. Put the eomuk on the skewers. • 소시지를 꼬치에 **끼우고** 밀가루를 뿌리세요. Put the sausage on the skewers and sprinkle with flour.
거르다 [georeuda]	to sift, to strain	• 건더기를 체에 **거르세요**. Strain out the solid ingredients. • 육수를 면포에 **걸러서** 식히세요. Strain the stock through cloth and then cool.
잠기다 [jamgida]	to submerge	• 어묵이 국물에 **잠기게** 하세요. Submerge the eomuk in the broth. • 건더기가 **잠길** 정도로 육수를 부으세요. Pour in enough stock to submerge the solid ingredients.

Let's Speak Korean!

Track 119

─○ 어떤 계절을 좋아해요?

A 어떤 계절을 좋아해요? Which season do you like?

B 저는 여름을 좋아해요. I like the summer.

어떤 is used when asking about the characteristics, content, or state of a person or thing, and is used in the form 어떤 N. The answer to 어떤 N~? can simply be "N + 요." The words for the seasons are 봄 (spring), 여름 (summer), 가을 (fall), and 겨울 (winter).

Exercise

A 어떤 고기를 좋아해요? Which kind of meat do you like?

B 저는 소고기를 좋아해요. I like beef.

A 어떤 과일을 좋아해요? Which fruits do you like?

B 사과를 좋아해요. I like apples.

─○ 따뜻한 어묵탕요.

Track 120

A 뭐 먹을까요? What shall we eat?

B 따뜻한 어묵탕요. Hot eomuktang.

–(으)ㄴ is an ending that allows an adjective to modify the noun that follows it.

Final consonant O + –은: 작(다) + –은 → 작은

Final consonant X / ㄹ + –ㄴ: 따뜻하(다) + ㄴ → 따뜻한

있다 / 없다 + –는: 맛있(다) + –는 → 맛있는

Be careful!

The ㄹ at the end of the stem of 달다 is removed when combined with ㄴ, ㅂ, ㅅ, or 오.

Ex 달(다) + ㄴ → 단

Exercise

A 어떤 음식을 좋아해요? Which foods do you like?

B 매운 음식을 좋아해요. I like spicy foods.

시원하다   달다

오징어볶음
Ojingeo-bokkeum

• OJINGEO-BOKKEUM •

Ojingeo-bokkeum is made of cleanly trimmed squid, onions, carrots, and other vegetables stir-fried with a seasoning of gochujang and red pepper powder. It is one of several spicy foods made with a basic seasoning of gochujang and red pepper powder, with Cheongyang chili pepper added in. Ojingeo-bokkeum is eaten as a side dish, but is also eaten on top of rice and mixed in a single bowl. When Korean people have little appetite, they often enjoy eating this type of spicy food.

재료 INGREDIENTS

2인분 Serves 2

오징어 1마리 (300g)
1 squid (300 grams)

양파 1/2개
1/2 onion

대파 50g
50 grams of green onion

당근 1/4개
1/4 carrot

풋고추 2개
2 green chili peppers

식용유 2큰술
2 tablespoons cooking oil

참기름 1큰술
1 tablespoon sesame oil

깨소금 1작은술
1 teaspoon ground sesame

Sauce & Marinade

볶음 양념장
MARINADE FOR STIR-FRY

고추장 1큰술
1 tablespoon gochujang

고춧가루 1큰술
1 tablespoon red pepper powder

간장 2큰술
2 tablespoons soy sauce

다진 마늘 1/2큰술
1/2 tablespoon crushed garlic

설탕 1큰술
1 tablespoon sugar

준비 PREPARATION

◆ 오징어는 내장과 뼈 등을 제거하고 껍질을 벗겨 준비한다.
Prepare the squid by removing the innards and bones, and peeling off the skin.

◆ 프라이팬은 깊은 팬을 사용하는 것이 편하다.
Using a deep frying pan is easier.

요리 COOKING

1 껍질을 벗긴 오징어는 1.5×5cm 정도 크기로 썬다.
Slice the peeled squid into 1.5×5 cm pieces.

2 당근은 1×4cm로 납작하게 썰고, 양파는 채를 썬다. 풋고추는 어슷썰기 하고, 대파는 반은 어슷썰기 하고 반은 송송 썰어 둔다.
Cut the carrot into flat 1×4 cm pieces and shred the onion. Slice the green chili peppers diagonally, and cut half the green onion diagonally and the other half into slices.

3 양념장 재료를 모두 섞어 볶음 양념장을 만들어 반으로 나누어 둔다.
Mix all the marinade ingredients to make the marinade for stir-fry and then split it in half.

4 팬에 불을 켜고 식용유, 송송 썬 대파를 넣어 볶으면서 파기름을 만든다.
Turn the heat on under a pan and make green onion oil by adding the sliced green onion to cooking oil and stir-frying.

5 대파가 노릇해지면 오징어와 양념장의 반만 넣는다. 1–2분 정도 볶다가 대파를 제외한 모든 채소와 남은 양념장을 넣고 같이 볶는다.
When the green onion browns, add the squid and the half of the marinade. Stir-fry for 1-2 minutes and add all the vegetables (except the diagonally cut green onion) and the remaining marinade and stir-fry together.

6 채소가 거의 다 익으면 대파를 넣고 1–2분쯤 더 볶는다. 불을 끄고 참기름을 넣고 섞은 후 그릇에 담고 깨소금을 뿌린다.
When the vegetables are nearly fully cooked, add the green onion and stir-fry for an additional 1-2 minutes. Turn off the heat, add the sesame oil, and after mixing, put in a bowl and sprinkle with ground sesame.

Track 121

재료 INGREDIENTS

오징어 [ojingeo]
squid

note
Squid, which has the highest protein content of any seafood, is used as an ingredient in stir-fries or soups, etc. Dried squid is roasted and eaten as a snack, and dried shredded squid is also stir-fried and made into a side dish.

풋고추 [putkkochu]
green chili pepper

note
Peppers are one of the most important ingredients in Korean food. Ripe red peppers are made into red pepper powder and gochujang, but young, unripe green chili peppers are also used as a spice in various dishes.

Track 122

요리 COOKING

Base Form	Meaning	Examples
벗기다 [beotkkida]	to peel	• 오징어는 껍질을 **벗기세요**. Peel off the skin of the squid. • 껍질을 **벗긴** 호두를 작게 다지세요. Chop the peeled walnuts into small pieces.
어슷썰다 [eoseutsseolda]	to cut/slice diagonally	• 가래떡을 **어슷써세요**. Cut the garaetteok diagonally. • 대파는 **어슷썰기** 하세요. Slice the green onion diagonally.
나누다 [nanuda]	to divide	• 표고버섯을 반으로 **나누세요**. Divide the shiitake mushrooms in half. • 양념장을 반씩 **나누어** 넣으세요. Divide the marinade in half and add it.

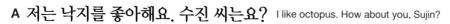
Let's Speak Korean!

─○ 오징어를 더 좋아해요.

Track 123

A 저는 낙지를 좋아해요. 수진 씨는요? I like octopus. How about you, Sujin?

B 저는 낙지보다 오징어를 더 좋아해요. I like squid more than octopus.

"N + 보다" is added to a word that is the target of a comparison, and is used when comparing two things. 더 gives the additional meaning of "more."

Ex 바나나보다 사과를 더 좋아해요.
단 음식보다 매운 음식을 좋아해요.

A 사과 좋아해요? Do you like apples?

B 사과보다 배를 좋아해요. I like pears more than apples.

A 삼계탕이랑 찜닭 중에 뭘 좋아해요? Which do you like, samgyetang or jjimdak?

B 찜닭보다 삼계탕을 더 좋아해요. I like samgyetang more than jjimdak.

─○ 맛있게 드세요.

Track 124

A 오징어볶음이에요. 맛있게 드세요. This is ojingeo-bokkeum. Enjoy your meal.

B 네, 고맙습니다. Thank you.

드시다 is the honorific form of 먹다 used when recommending that the other party try eating some food. 맛있게 드세요 (literally, "Eat deliciously.") is a common greeting used before eating a meal.

A 맛있게 드세요. Enjoy your meal.

B 네, 잘 먹겠습니다. Thank you for the meal. (literally, "I'll eat well.")

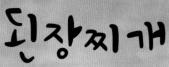

된장찌개
Doenjangjjigae

• DOENJANGJJIGAE •

Doenjang is made from the solid ingredients that remain after soy beans are
boiled, fermented, and soaked in soy sauce. Doenjangjjigae is a soup made
by beating doenjang into water; adding Korean squash, onion, and other
vegetables, meat, tofu, etc.; and boiling together. There are no set ingredients,
and as long as you have doenjang, any ingredients you combine will be made
into a delicious doenjangjjigae. It is a dish that reminds
Korean people of "home cooking" and is a typical Korean food.

재료 INGREDIENTS

2-3인분 Serves 2-3

소고기 100g
100 grams of beef

두부 1/3모 (80g)
1/3 block (80 grams) of tofu

무 50g
50 grams of radish

호박 30g
30 grams of Korean squash

양파 1/2개
1/2 onion

풋고추 1개
1 green chili pepper

대파 30g
30 grams of green onion

된장 1½큰술
1 ½ tablespoons soybean paste

다진 마늘 1작은술
1 teaspoon crushed garlic

고춧가루 1작은술
1 teaspoon red pepper powder

물 2컵
2 cups of water

준비 PREPARATION

◆ 소고기는 어떤 부위든 괜찮으며, 한입 크기로 썬다.
Any cut of beef can be used. Cut into bite-sized pieces.

◆ 된장은 '된장' 또는 '재래식 된장'을 사용해야 되며, '쌈장'은 색깔은 비슷하지만 전혀 다른 것이라서 찌개에는 사용할 수 없다.
Regular doenjang or traditional doenjang should be used. Ssamjang is a similar color but a completely different ingredient and cannot be used in stews.

요리 COOKING

1 소고기와 두부는 한입 크기로 썰고, 호박은 반달썰기, 양파는 채썰기 한다. 무는 얇게 나박썰기 하고, 풋고추와 대파는 어슷썰기 한다.
Cut the beef and tofu into bite-sized pieces, cut the Korean squash into half-moon slices, and shred the onion. Slice the radish into thin rectangles and slice the green chili pepper and green onion diagonally.

2 냄비에 소고기를 넣고 약불에서 서서히 볶으며 익힌다.
Add the beef to a pot and cook by stir-frying slowly over low heat.

3 고기가 익으면 물을 붓고 된장을 푼다.
When the beef is cooked, pour in the water and beat in the doenjang.

4 무를 넣고 약불로 10분 정도 끓인다.
Add the radish and boil over low heat for 10 minutes.

5 무가 익으면 호박, 양파, 두부, 풋고추, 고춧가루, 다진 마늘을 넣고 5분 정도 끓인다.
When the radish is cooked, add the squash, onion, tofu, green chili pepper, red pepper powder, and crushed garlic, and boil for 5 minutes.

6 부족한 간은 된장으로 하며, 마지막에 대파를 넣고 1분쯤 더 끓인다.
Add doenjang if the flavor is insufficient, then add green onion at the end and boil for about 1 more minute.

Track 125

재료 INGREDIENTS

된장 [doenjang]
doenjang (soybean paste)

note
Doenjang is a traditional Korean ingredient made by boiling and fermenting soy beans, and is a typical fermented food. In a Korean person's diet, which was mostly centered around rice and vegetables, It is also a food that served as a source of protein.

애호박 [aehobak]
(Korean) squash

note
This can be called "Korean squash" and is a different type of squash from zucchini. It is widely used in doenjangjjigae, and is also used in seasoned vegetables, jeon, etc.

Track 126

요리 COOKING

Base Form	Meaning	Examples
다르다 [dareuda]	to be different	• 쌈장과 된장은 **달라요.** Ssamjang and doenjang are different. • 어제 먹은 것과 **다른** 것을 먹고 싶어요. I want to eat something different from what I ate yesterday.
없다 [eoptta]	to not be, to not have	• 쌈장은 된장찌개에 사용할 수 **없어요.** Ssamjang cannot be used in doenjangjjigae. • 감자가 **없어서** 슈퍼마켓에 가요. I don't have potatoes so I'm going to the supermarket.
부족하다 [bujokada]	to be insufficient, to be not enough	• 간이 **부족하면** 된장을 넣으세요. If the taste is insufficient, add doenjang. • 국물이 좀 **부족해요.** There isn't quite enough broth.

Let's Speak Korean!

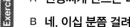

─○ 10분쯤 걸려요.

Track 127

A 빨리 만들 수 있어요? Can you make it quickly?

B 네, 10분쯤 걸려요. Yes, it takes about 10 minutes.

쯤 is a word that gives the additional meaning of an approximate amount and corresponds to "about." The 분 in 10분 is a unit for reading time and means "minutes."

Ex 20분쯤   1마리쯤   하루쯤

A 된장찌개 만드는 데 얼마나 걸려요? How long does it take to make doenjangjjigae?

B 네, 이십 분쯤 걸려요. It takes about 20 minutes.

15분쯤 (십오 분쯤)	30분쯤 (삼십 분쯤)
45분쯤 (사십오 분쯤)	50분쯤 (오십 분쯤)

─○ 된장찌개를 끓이고 있어요.

Track 128

A 뭐 하고 있어요? What are you doing?

B 된장찌개를 끓이고 있어요. I'm boiling doenjangjjigae.

–고 있다 is an expression that indicates something is in progress. It is used in the form of "V + –고 있다" and has the same meaning as –(으)ㄴ 중이다.

Ex 만들(다) + –고 있어요 → 만들고 있어요
요리하(다) + –고 있어요 → 요리하고 있어요

A 뭐 해요? What are you doing?

B 저녁밥을 준비하고 있어요. I'm preparing dinner.

양파를 씻다	설거지하다	대파를 썰다

부대찌개

Budaejjigae

• BUDAEJJIAGE •

Budaejjigae is a food made by putting kimchi, sausage, ham, and various vegetables in a pot, pouring in stock, adding marinade, and boiling. As you can already tell from the ingredients, it is not a traditional Korean food, but rather was created during the Korean War when sausage and spam arrived through American army bases. The kimchi creates a unique combination with the sausage and ham, so it is spicy and also allows you to taste the deep flavor of the broth from the meat.

재료 INGREDIENTS

3-4인분 Serves 3-4

김치 100g
100 grams of kimchi

다진 소고기 60g
60 grams of ground beef

햄 100g
100 grams of ham

소시지 4개 4 sausages

떡국떡 50g
50 grams of tteokguktteok

두부 1/2모 1/2 block of tofu

양파 1/2개 1/2 onion

대파 50g
50 grams of green onion

슬라이스 치즈 1장
1 slice of cheese

라면 사리 1개
1 pack of instant noodles

물 (또는 고기 육수) 4컵
4 cups of water (or meat stock)

베이크드빈 3큰술
(생략 가능)
3 tablespoons baked beans (can
be omitted)

Sauce & Marinade

고기 양념 MEAT SEASONING

간장 1/2큰술
1/2 tablespoon soy sauce
다진 마늘 1작은술
1 teaspoon crushed garlic
후춧가루 조금
a pinch of ground black pepper

양념장 MARINADE

고추장 2큰술
2 tablespoons gochujang
고춧가루 2큰술
2 tablespoons red pepper powder
간장 2큰술
2 tablespoons soy sauce
다진 마늘 1큰술
1 tablespoon crushed garlic
후춧가루
ground black pepper

준비 PREPARATION

◆ 육수는 소고기를 넣고 중약불에서 30분 이상 끓여 만들 수 있으며, 시중에서 판매
하는 사골 육수, 곰탕 등을 사용해도 좋다.
You can make the stock by adding beef and boiling over medium-low heat for 30 minutes or
more, and you can also use beef bone broth or soup, etc. that is sold at the market.

◆ 신김치를 사용해야 맛이 좋으며, 떡국떡, 베이크드빈, 치즈는 생략해도 된다.
Sour kimchi should be used for the best taste, and the tteokguktteok, baked beans, and
cheese can be omitted.

요리 COOKING

1 두부, 소시지, 햄은 먹기 좋은 크기로 썰고, 김치는 소를 털어내고 먹기 좋은 크
기로 썬다. Cut the tofu, sausage, and ham into pieces a good size for eating. Remove the
kimchi filling and cut the kimchi into pieces a good size for eating.

2 양파는 굵게 채를 썰고, 대파는 어슷썰기 한다. 떡국떡은 씻어 둔다.
Shred the onion into thick pieces and slice the green onion diagonally. Wash the tteokguktteok and set aside.

3 다진 소고기는 고기 양념을 넣고 고루 섞어서 10분 정도 재워 둔다.
Add the meat seasoning to the ground beef and mix evenly, then leave to sit for 10 minutes.

4 볼에 양념장 재료를 모두 넣고 잘 섞는다.
Add all the marinade ingredients to a bowl and mix well.

5 냄비에 모든 재료를 담고 양념장을 올린 후 물이나 육수를 냄비에 맞게 붓고 끓인
다. 양념장을 육수 양에 따라 넣고 남겨 둔다. Put all the ingredients in a pot and after
adding the marinade on top, pour water or stock to match the size of the pot and boil. Add
marinade depending on the amount of stock and save whatever is left over.

6 국물이 5분 정도 끓고 나면 라면 사리와 치즈를 넣고 기호에 따라 양념장을 더하
여 라면이 익을 때까지 더 끓인다. After boiling the soup for 5 minutes, add the instant
noodles and cheese, add more marinade according to your preferences, and continue to boil until the instant noodles are cooked.

Track 129

재료 INGREDIENTS

라면 사리 [ramyeon sari]
instant noodles

note
This refers only the noodles from packs of instant noodles, without the soup. As more and more people are adding them to budaejjigae, tteokbokki, etc., the noodles on their own are sold separately.

떡국떡 [tteokguktteok]
tteokguktteok

note
Hardened garaetteok cut diagonally are used when boiling tteokguk, but lately, are often added as an additional ingredient to other dishes.

Track 130

요리 COOKING

Base Form	Meaning	Examples
털어내다 [teoreonaeda]	to shake off, to clean off	• 뭉쳐진 밀가루를 **털어내고** 달걀물을 입히세요. Shake off the lumps of flour and dredge in egg mixture. • 야채의 물기를 **털어내세요**. Shake the water off of the vegetables.
남기다 [namgida]	to leave	• 양념장을 조금 **남기세요**. Leave a little bit of marinade. • **남겨** 둔 국물을 더 부으세요. Pour in more of the left aside broth.
더하다 [deohada]	to add (up)	• 치즈를 **더하면** 맛있어요. It's delicious if you add cheese. • 싱거우면 양념장을 **더하세요**. If it's bland, add marinade.

Let's Speak Korean!

Track 131

물을 많이 넣으면 안 돼요.

A 물을 더 넣어도 돼요? Can we add more water?

B 아니요, 물을 많이 넣으면 안 돼요. No, we can't add too much water.

"A/V + −(으)면 안 되다" indicates that a certain action is prohibited or restricted.

> Final consonant O + −으면 안 돼요: 넣(다) + −으면 안 돼요 → 넣으면 안 돼요
>
> Final consonant X / ㄹ + −면 안 돼요: 남기(다) + −면 안 돼요 → 남기면 안 돼요
> 갈(다) + −면 안 돼요 → 갈면 안 돼요

✦ 냄비 뚜껑을 <u>열면 안 돼요</u>. The lid of the pot can't be opened.

✦ 불이 <u>세면 안 돼요</u>. The heat can't be too strong.

✦ 국물이 끓기 전에 <u>먹으면 안 돼요</u>. The soup can't be eaten before it boils.

Track 132

국물이 끓으면 파를 넣으세요.

A 파는 언제 넣어요? When do I add the green onion?

B 국물이 끓으면 파를 넣으세요. Add the green onion when the soup boils.

"A/V + −(으)면" is an ending that indicates conditions or assumptions regarding the following clause.

> Final consonant O + −으면: 끓(다) + −으면 → 끓으면
>
> Final consonant X / ㄹ + −면: 더하(다) + −면 → 더하면
> 달(다) + −면 → 달면

✦ 양념장을 <u>더하면</u> 더 맛있어요. If you add more marinade, it's more delicious.

✦ 국물이 <u>끓으면</u> 라면 사리를 넣으세요. When the soup boils, add the instant noodles.

✦ 달걀이 반쯤 <u>익으면</u> 말아 주세요. When the eggs are half cooked, roll them.

잡채
Japchae

• JAPCHAE •

This is a food made with boiled glass noodles; stir-fried vegetables such as
spinach, carrots, and onion; and meat; eaten mixed with soy sauce seasoning.
As each ingredient is seasoned and cooked before being mixed, the texture
of each is retained, and the taste of the glass noodles and the vegetables go
together well. Because it has long been considered a bright and elegant dish,
It is an indispensible food on the table at various celebrations such as
birthday parties, wedding receptions, etc.

재료 INGREDIENTS

2-3인분 Serves 2-3

당면 250g
250 grams of glass noodles

돼지고기 100g
100 grams of pork

시금치 150g
150 grams of spinach

양파 1개
1 onion

당근 1/2개
1/2 carrot

목이버섯 3g
3 grams of wood ear mushrooms

간장 4큰술
4 tablespoons soy sauce

설탕 2큰술
2 tablespoons sugar

참기름 3큰술
3 tablespoons sesame oil

소금 1큰술
1 tablespoon salt

후춧가루 조금
a pinch of ground black pepper

통깨 1/2큰술
1/2 tablespoon sesame seeds

식용유 4큰술
4 tablespoons cooking oil

> **TIPS**
>
> * Shiitake mushrooms or oyster mushrooms can also be used instead of wood ear mushrooms.

준비 PREPARATION

◆ 당면과 목이버섯은 미리 물에 불린다.
   Soak the glass noodles and wood ear mushrooms in water first.

◆ 시금치는 뿌리를 제거하고 한 줄기씩 뜯어 끓는 물에 살짝 데친다.
   Remove the roots of the spinach, tear off leaf by leaf, and blanch slightly in boiling water.

요리 COOKING

1 돼지고기, 당근, 양파는 길게 채를 썬다. 목이버섯은 한입 크기로 자른다.
Shred the pork, carrot, and onion into long pieces. Cut the wood ear mushrooms into bite-sized pieces.

2 데친 시금치에 간장 1/3큰술을 넣고 무친다.
Add 1/3 tablespoon soy sauce to the blanched spinach and mix.

3 당근, 양파, 목이버섯, 돼지고기는 각각 달군 팬에 기름을 두르고 소금과 후춧가루를 약간씩 넣고 볶는다.
In a pan coated with oil, stir-fry the carrot, onion, wood ear mushrooms, and pork, each separately, with a little bit of salt and ground black pepper added.

4 불린 당면은 끓는 물에 삶아 찬물에 헹군다. 헹군 당면은 물기를 제거하고 먹기 좋게 자른다.
Boil the soaked glass noodles in boiling water then rinse with cold water. Remove water from the rinsed glass noodles and cut into a length a good size for eating.

5 볼에 당면과 볶은 재료, 시금치를 넣고 참기름, 설탕, 후춧가루, 간장을 넣고 골고루 섞어 준다. 간장의 양은 입맛에 맞추어 조절한다.
Add the glass noodles, stir-fried ingredients, and spinach to a bowl, add sesame oil, sugar, ground black pepper, and soy sauce, and mix evenly. Adjust the amount of soy sauce to taste.

6 접시에 잡채를 담고 통깨를 뿌려 마무리한다.
Put the japchae on a plate and finish by sprinkling with sesame seeds.

Track 133

재료 INGREDIENTS

당면 [dangmyeon]
glass noodles

note
Because they are made with sweet potato starch, glass noodles have a chewier texture than other noodles. As an essential ingredient for japchae, they are also used in broths, soups, etc.

목이버섯 [mogibeoseot]
wood ear mushroom

note
As a type of mushroom that grows as a parasite on trees, it has the name "wood ear" because its shape resembles the shape of a person's ear. Wood ear mushrooms are used in japchae, other stir-fry dishes, etc.

Track 134

요리 COOKING

Base Form	Meaning	Examples
길다 [gilda]	to be long	• 양파는 **길게** 채를 썰어요. Shred the onion into long pieces. • 당근 채가 너무 **길어요**. The shredded carrots are too long.
끓다 [kkeulta]	to boil	• 시금치를 **끓는** 물에 데치세요. Blanch the spinach in boiling water. • 국물이 **끓으면** 채소를 넣으세요. When the broth boils, add the vegetables.
조절하다 [jojeolhada]	to adjust	• 기호에 맞게 간장의 양을 **조절하세요**. Adjust the amount of soy sauce according to your preferences. • 재료의 양에 따라 간장의 양을 **조절해야 돼요**. You should adjust the amount of soy sauce depending on the amount of ingredients.

Let's Speak Korean!

Track 135

⟜ 생일 파티를 할 거예요.

A 내일 뭐 할 거예요? What will you do tomorrow?

B 생일 파티를 할 거예요. I'll have a birthday party tomorrow.

"V + –(으)ㄹ 거예요" is an expression used when indicating an event or action that will occur in the future.

> Final consonant O + –을 거예요: 볶(다) + –을 거예요 → 볶을 거예요
> Final consonant X + –ㄹ 거예요: 끓이(다) + –ㄹ 거예요 → 끓일 거예요

Exercise

A 점심에 메뉴는 뭐예요? What's the menu for lunch?

B 갈비탕을 끓일 거예요. I'll boil galbitang.

> 새우전을 부치다   돼지고기를 삶다

⟜ 식은 후에 넣으세요.

Track 136

A 당면을 지금 넣을까요? Shall I add the glass noodles now?

B 식은 후에 넣으세요. Add them after they cool.

"V + –(으)ㄴ 후에" is an expression used when something is followed by another action.

> Final consonant O + –은 후에: 식(다) + –은 후에 → 식은 후에
> Final consonant X + –ㄴ 후에: 끄(다) + –ㄴ 후에 → 끈 후에

Exercise

A 이건 언제 넣어요? When do I add this?

B 불을 끈 후에 넣으세요. Add it after turning off the heat.

> 국물이 끓다   감자가 익다

159

김말이
Gimmari

· GIMMARI ·

Gimmari is a type of fried food and is made by rolling glass noodles and
various vegetables in laver, dredging in batter, and deep-frying.
Along with tteokbokki and kkochi-eomuk, they are a snack that can
easily be eaten at street stalls or snack bars, and the taste is
superior when they are eaten dipped in tteokbokki sauce rather than
on its own. At home, it can be made easily if there is
leftover japchae by rolling this dish up as is in laver,
and they are often made and eaten with tteokbokki.

재료 INGREDIENTS

3-4인분 Serves 3-4

김 4장
4 sheets of laver

당면 100g
100 grams of glass noodles

양파 1/2개
1/2 onion

당근 1/3개
1/3 carrot

간장 1½큰술
1 ½ tablespoons soy sauce

설탕 1/2큰술
1/2 tablespoon sugar

참기름 1/2큰술
1/2 tablespoon sesame oil

소금 1/2 작은술
1/2 teaspoon salt

후춧가루 조금
a pinch of ground black pepper

튀김 가루 1½컵
1 ⅓ cups of frying mix

물 1컵
1 cup of water

식용유 약간
a little cooking oil

Tips

* If you add ice to the deep-fry batter, the fried rolls will become crispier.

준비 PREPARATION

♦ 김은 김밥 김을 준비하고 4등분으로 자른다.
Prepare laver for gimbap and cut into quarters.

♦ 남은 잡채가 있다면 살짝 볶거나 전자레인지에 데워서 만들면 된다.
If there is any leftover japchae, you can stir-fry it lightly or heat in the microwave.

요리 COOKING

1 당면은 미리 물에 불려 두었다가 끓는 물에 삶아서 찬물에 헹구어 3-4등분으로 자른다.
Soak the glass noodles in water beforehand and leave to sit, then boil in boiling water, rinse in cold water, and cut into thirds or quarters.

2 당근과 양파는 채를 썰어, 한꺼번에 프라이팬에 소금과 후추를 조금 넣고 살짝 볶아 식힌다.
Shred the carrot and onion, add them at the same time to a frying pan with a little salt and ground black pepper, lightly stir-fry, and leave to cool down.

3 볼에 당면, 당근, 양파, 간장, 설탕, 참기름을 넣고 골고루 섞는다.
Add the glass noodles, carrot, onion, soy sauce, sugar, and sesame oil to a bowl and mix evenly.

4 자른 김을 펼쳐서 양념한 당면을 넣고 말은 후 마지막에 물을 살짝 묻혀 붙인다.
Spread out the cut laver, add the seasoned glass noodles, then after rolling, finish by coating with a little water and sticking together.

5 말아 둔 김말이는 튀김 가루를 묻혀 둔다.
Coat the rolled up gimmari in frying mix and set aside.

6 튀김 가루와 물을 1:1로 섞어 튀김 반죽을 만들고, 김말이에 튀김 반죽을 입혀 노릇하게 튀긴다.
Mix the frying mix with water in a 1:1 ratio to make deep-fry batter, dredge the gimmari in the deep-fry batter, and deep-fry to golden brown.

Vocabulary

Track 137

재료 INGREDIENTS

튀김 가루 [twigim garu]
frying mix

note
It is a type of mix used when deep-frying. In order to make crispy deep-fried foods, it uses a soft flour with a low gluten content.

물 [mul]
water

note
In Korea, tap water can be used as is for cooking, but purchased bottled water is also used frequently.

Track 138

요리 COOKING

Base Form	Meaning	Examples
식히다 [sikida]	to cool down	• 당면을 삶아서 **식히세요**. Boil and cool the glass noodles. • **식힌** 찹쌀 풀을 양념과 섞으세요. Mix the cooled down glutinous rice paste with the seasoning.
펼치다 [pyeolchida]	to spread out	• 김을 **펼치고** 당면을 놓으세요. Spread out the laver and add the glass noodles. • **펼쳐진** 밥 위에 재료를 얹으세요. Put the ingredients on top of the spread-out rice.
튀기다 [twigida]	to deep-fry	• 김말이를 노릇하게 **튀기세요**. Deep-fry the gimmari to golden brown. • 핫도그를 **튀겨서** 기름을 빼세요. Deep-fry the Korean-style hot dog and remove the oil.

Let's Speak Korean!

—○ 버리지 마세요.

A 잡채가 많이 남았어요. There's a lot of japchae left over.

B 버리지 마세요. 김말이를 만드세요. Don't throw that out. Make gimmari.

Track 139

"V + −지 말다" is an expression used when making it so that an action will not be performed or when stopping an action.

Ex 버리(다) + −지 마세요 → 버리지 마세요
널리(다) + −지 마세요 → 넣지 마세요

Exercise
- ✦ 소금을 넣지 마세요. Don't add salt.
- ✦ 당면은 볶지 마세요. Don't stir-fry the glass noodles.
- ✦ 깨소금을 뿌리지 마세요. Don't sprinkle with ground sesame.

—○ 떡볶이하고 같이 드세요.

A 김말이만 먹어요? Should I eat just the gimmari?

B 김말이는 떡볶이하고 같이 드세요. 더 맛있어요.
Eat the gimmari with tteokbokki. It's more delicious.

Track 140

"같이," which means that 2 or more people or things are together, has the meaning of "with" and is used in front of a verb. 드시다 is an honorific expression for 먹다 (to eat).

Ex 양파는 당근과 같이 볶아요. 소금과 후추를 같이 넣어요.

Exercise
A 감자는 어떻게 해요? What do I do with the potatoes?

B 감자는 호박과 같이 볶아요. Stir-fry the potatoes with the Korean squash.

같이 넣다	같이 삶다	같이 끓이다

호떡
Hotteok

◆ HOTTEOK ◆

Hotteok is a type of snack food made by fermenting a flour dough, adding a
filling of dark brown sugar and nuts, and frying in a well-oiled pan.
When you bite into a hotteok cooked with a browned and crispy exterior,
the black sugar filling spreads sweetly in your mouth, like chocolate or
caramel. Hotteok is one of many street food snacks, and is more popular
in the winter. Nowadays, the number of unique types, such as seed-stuffed
hotteok, green tea hotteok, etc., has increased.

재료 INGREDIENTS

2-3인분 Serves 2-3

반죽 DOUGH

밀가루 200g
200 grams of flour

설탕 15g
15 grams of sugar

소금 1g
1 gram of salt

이스트 4g
4 grams of yeast

미지근한 물 150ml
150 milliliters of lukewarm water

식용유 1큰술
1 tablespoon cooking oil

호떡 소 HOTTEOK FILLING

흑설탕 80g
80 grams of dark brown sugar

계핏가루 1작은술
1 teaspoon cinnamon powder

견과류 50g (땅콩, 호두 등)
50 grams of nuts (peanuts, walnuts, etc.)

식용유 적당량
a good amount of cooking oil

TIPS

* These taste even better when ice cream is placed on top of the freshly made hotteok.

준비 PREPARATION

◆ 호떡 소에 들어가는 설탕은 흑설탕을 사용해야 맛과 향을 낼 수 있다.
The sugar in the hotteok filling should be dark brown sugar to produce the taste and aroma.

◆ 견과류는 땅콩, 호두, 피칸 등 어떤 종류도 괜찮으며 두 가지 이상의 견과류를 섞어도 좋다.
For the nuts, peanuts, walnuts, pecans, etc. can all be used, and it is good to mix two or more types together.

요리 COOKING

1 견과류를 잘게 다져 흑설탕, 계핏가루와 섞어서 소를 만든다.
Finely chop the nuts and mix with dark brown sugar and cinnamon powder to make the filling.

2 미지근한 물에 이스트를 넣고 완전히 녹을 때까지 잘 저어 준다.
Add yeast to lukewarm water and mix until completely dissolved.

3 볼에 밀가루, 설탕, 소금, 식용유 1큰술과 이스트 녹인 물을 넣어 반죽을 한다. 반죽이 2배쯤 될 때까지 따뜻한 곳에서 발효시킨다.
Add flour, sugar, salt, 1 tablespoon cooking oil, and the dissolved yeast water to a bowl to make the dough. Ferment the dough in a warm place until it has doubled in size.

4 손에 식용유를 바르고 반죽을 펼쳐 소를 1큰술 넣고 오므린다.
Coat your hands in cooking oil, spread the dough, add 1 tablespoon of filling, and close.

5 팬을 달군 후 기름을 넉넉히 두르고 오므린 부분이 아래쪽으로 되도록 호떡을 올려 중약불에서 굽는다.
After heating the pan, coat with plenty of oil and place the hotteok with the closure face-down, then fry over medium-low heat.

6 아래쪽 겉면이 노릇하면 뒤집어서 호떡을 눌러 주고 양면을 뒤집으며 완전히 익힌다.
When the outside of the bottom is golden brown, flip and press down on the hotteok, then continue to flip while cooking until done.

Vocabulary

재료 INGREDIENTS

Track 141

흑설탕 [heuksseoltang]
dark brown sugar

note

Dark brown sugar has the unique flavor of raw sugar and is tinged with a deep color. It is therefore often used in traditional sweets like yaksik, sujeonggwa, yakgwa, etc.

계핏가루 [gyepitkkaru]
cinnamon powder

note

Cinnamon powder, or finely ground cinnamon, is one of the top three spices in the world, along with black pepper and cloves. Cinnamon powder is used in tteok filling, and cinnamon is used to make sujeonggwa (cinnamon punch).

요리 COOKING

Track 142

Base Form	Meaning	Examples
잘다 [jalda]	to be small	• 견과류를 **잘게** 다지세요. Chop the nuts into small pieces. • 이번에 산 감자는 너무 **잘아요**. The potatoes I bought this time are too small.
발효시키다 [balhyosikida]	to ferment	• 반죽을 30분 **발효시켜요**. Ferment the dough for 30 minutes. • 김치와 된장은 **발효시킨** 음식이에요. Kimchi and doenjang are fermented foods.
오므리다 [omeurida]	to close up, to purse closed	• 소를 넣고 반죽을 **오므리세요**. Add the filling and purse closed the dough. • 만두소를 넣고 반죽을 **오므린** 다음 모양을 만드세요. Add the mandu filling and, after closing up the dough, shape the mandu.

Let's Speak Korean!

─○ 흑설탕과 견과류로 만들어요.

Track 143

A 호떡 소는 뭐로 만들어요? What is hotteok filling made with?

B 흑설탕과 견과류로 만들어요. It's made with dark brown sugar and nuts.

"N + (으)로" is a postpositional particle attached after a noun and is used when indicating the ingredients or materials of something.

> Final consonant O + 으로: 닭 + 으로 → 닭으로
>
> Final consonant X / ㄹ + 로: 우유 + 로 → 우유로   달걀 + 로 → 달걀로

Ex 삼계탕은 닭으로 만든다.   치즈는 우유로 만든다.

Exercise

A **이거 뭐로 만든 거예요?** What is this made with?

B **감자로 만든 거예요.** It's made with potatoes.

| 닭고기 | 된장 | 김치 | 순두부 | 미역 |

─○ 집에서 만들 수 있어요.

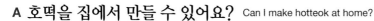
Track 144

A 호떡을 집에서 만들 수 있어요? Can I make hotteok at home?

B 네, 집에서 만들 수 있어요. Yes, you can make them at home.

"V + −(으)ㄹ 수 있어요" is an expression that indicates an action is possible.

> Final consonant O + −을 수 있어요: 먹(다) + −을 수 있어요 → 먹을 수 있어요
>
> Final consonant X + −ㄹ 수 있어요: 요리하(다) + −ㄹ 수 있어요 → 요리할 수 있어요

Exercise

✦ 매운 음식을 먹을 수 있어요. I can eat spicy food.

✦ 한국 음식을 요리할 수 있어요. I can cook Korean food.

✦ 짜파구리를 끓일 수 있어요. I can make jjapaguri.

감자전
Gamjajeon

• GAMJAJEON •

Gamjajeon is a food made by finely grating raw potatoes with a grater, adding the solid matter and settled starch, making a batter, and frying in oil.
Not many ingredients are used and the method of making the jeon is simple, so it can be easily made and eaten at home. Along with kimchijeon and nokdujeon (mung bean pancakes), savory and chewy gamjajeon is a snack and side dish that call to mind a rainy day. For a refreshing and spicy taste, they are also made together with green chili peppers, onion, etc.

재료 INGREDIENTS

2-3인분 Serves 2-3

감자 3개 (400g)
3 potatoes (400 grams)

소금 1/2작은술
1/2 teaspoon salt

식용유 4큰술
4 tablespoons cooking oil

홍고추 또는 풋고추1/2개
(생략 가능)
1/2 red chili pepper or green chili
pepper (can be omitted)

Sauce & Marinade

초간장
SOY SAUCE AND VINEGAR MIX

간장 1큰술
1 tablespoon soy sauce

식초 1큰술
1 tablespoon vinegar

물 1/2큰술
1/2 tablespoon water

풋고추 1/2개 (생략 가능)
1/2 green chili pepper (can be
omitted)

준비 PREPARATION

◆ 감자는 갈아서 사용할 것이기 때문에 큰 것이 편하다.
Because the potatoes are for grating, bigger ones are more convenient.

요리 COOKING

1 감자는 껍질을 까고 강판에 갈아서 짜지 말고 체에 밭쳐서 수분과 건더기를 분리
한다.
Peel the potato skins off, grate the potatoes with a grater, and without squeezing, separate
the liquid from the solids by straining them through a sieve.

2 풋고추는 어슷썰기 하고 초간장 재료를 섞어 썰어 놓은 고추를 1-2개 띄운다.
Slice the green chili pepper diagonally, mix the soy sauce and vinegar mix ingredients, and
float 1-2 slices of the pepper on top.

3 감자에서 나온 물을 잠시 그대로 두었다가 전분이 가라앉으면 윗물을 따라 버린다.
Leave the potato liquid as is for a moment, and when the starch sinks, pour out the liquid
on top.

4 전분과 갈아 놓은 감자, 소금을 골고루 섞어 반죽을 만든다.
Mix the starch and the grated potatoes evenly with salt to make a batter.

5 프라이팬에 기름을 두르고 반죽을 한 국자씩 떠서 동그랗게 펴고 어슷썰기 한
고추를 올려 장식한다.
Coat a frying pan in oil, pour in one ladle of batter at a time, spread into a circle, and decorate
by placing the diagonally sliced green chili pepper on top.

6 중약불에서 앞뒤로 뒤집어 가며 노릇하게 지져, 초간장을 곁들여 낸다.
Over medium-low heat, fry to golden brown while turning over, then serve with the soy
sauce and vinegar mix.

Vocabulary

Track 145

재료 INGREDIENTS

감자 [gamja]
potato

note
Potatoes are eaten boiled or roasted, but are also used as a main or minor ingredient in various dishes including stir-fries, braised dishes, stews, soups, etc.

식초 [sikcho]
vinegar

note
Vinegar is usually used as a seasoning, but is also added to seasoned raw vegetables, gochujang, soy sauce, etc. to enhance the flavor.

Track 146

요리 COOKING

Base Form	Meaning	Examples
까다 [kkada]	to peel	• 감자는 껍질을 **까고** 강판에 가세요. Peel the potato skins off and grate the potatoes with a grater. • 마늘 껍질을 **까세요**. Peel the skin of the garlic.
밭치다 [batchida]	to strain	• 강판에 간 감자를 체에 **밭치세요**. Strain the grated potatoes through a sieve. • 씻은 야채를 체에 **밭쳐서** 물기를 빼세요. Strain the washed vegetables in a sieve to remove the water.
두르다 [dureuda]	to oil, to grease, to coat	• 프라이팬에 식용유를 **두르세요**. Coat the frying pan with cooking oil. • 식용유를 **두른** 팬에 반죽을 얹으세요. Put the batter in a pan greased with cooking oil.

Let's Speak Korean!

🔑 감자를 사러 가요.

Track 147

A 어디에 가요? Where are you going?

B 감자를 사러 가요. I'm going to buy potatoes.

"V + -(으)러 가다" is an expression used when indicating the reason or purpose for going somewhere.

> Final consonant O + -으러 가요: 먹(다) + -으러 → 먹<u>으러</u> 가요
>
> Final consonant X / ㄹ + -러 가요: 사(다) + -러 → 사<u>러</u> 가요
>
> 놀(다) + -러 → 놀<u>러</u> 가요

Exercise

A 어디에 가요? Where are you going?

B <u>저녁을 먹으러</u> 가요. I'm going to eat dinner.

파티를 하다	친구를 만나다

🔑 감자가 얼마예요?

Track 148

A 감자가 얼마예요? How much are potatoes?

B 100g에 육백 원이에요. They're 600 won for 100g.

얼마예요? is an expression used when asking the price of an item. The 에 in 100g에 means "for" or "per," and when reading prices, Sino-Korean numbers are used.

Ex 680원: 육백팔십 원   1,300원: 천삼백 원

       78,000원: 칠만 팔천 원   594,000원: 오십구만 사천 원

Exercise

A 식초 1병에 얼마예요? How much is 1 bottle of vinegar?

B <u>이천팔백 원</u>이에요. It's 2,800 won.

3,800원 (삼천팔백 원)	1,600원 (천육백 원)	4,700원 (사천칠백 원)

171

호박죽
Hobakjuk

• HOBAKJUK •

Hobakjuk is made by boiling and mashing pumpkins, adding glutinous rice flour, and boiling into a porridge. The fine golden color and the gentle, sweet taste delight the eyes and mouth. In the past, each house grew their own pumpkins and the fruit, leaves, and shoots were all cooked in various ways and eaten. As hobakjuk is mild and light, it is eaten as a breakfast, snack, or appetizer. It is low in calories and is used as a diet food, as well.

재료 INGREDIENTS

3-4인분 Serves 3-4

늙은 호박 (또는 단호박) 600g
600 grams of pumpkin (or butter-cup squash)

강낭콩 (또는 팥) 1/2컵
1/2 cup of kidney beans (or red beans)

찹쌀가루 3큰술
3 tablespoons glutinous rice flour

설탕 2큰술
2 tablespoons sugar

소금 1작은술
1 teaspoon salt

물 4컵
4 cups of water

준비 PREPARATION

◆ 호박죽은 보통 늙은 호박으로 만들지만 단호박을 사용할 수도 있다.
Hobakjuk is usually made with ordinary pumpkin. Buttercup squash can also be used.

요리 COOKING

  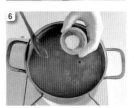

1 강낭콩 또는 팥은 불렸다가 냄비에 물을 넉넉히 붓고 무르도록 40분 정도 삶는다. 팥을 삶을 때에는 10분 정도 끓이다가 끓이던 물을 버리고 다시 물을 붓고 끓여야 한다.
After soaking the kidney beans or red beans, pour a generous amount of water into a pot and boil for 40 minutes to soften. When boiling the red beans, you should boil for 10 minutes, pour out the boiling water, then pour more water in and boil again.

2 호박은 전자레인지에 2분 정도 돌린 후 자른다. 호박의 속을 파내고 껍질을 벗겨 큼직하게 썬다. (단호박도 같은 방법으로 준비한다.)
Cut the pumpkin after heating for 2 minutes in the microwave. Hollow out the inside, remove the skin, and cut into large pieces. (Prepare the buttercup squash in the same way.)

3 손질한 호박과 물 3컵을 넣고 믹서기에 곱게 간다.
Add 3 cups of water to the prepared pumpkin and grind finely in a blender.

4 찹쌀가루에 물1컵을 넣고 덩어리가 생기지 않도록 풀어 준다.
Add 1 cup of water to glutinous rice flour and beat to prevent clumping.

5 냄비에 간 호박을 넣고 중약불에서 저어가며 끓이다가 끓어오르면, 찹쌀가루 푼 물, 강낭콩, 설탕을 넣고 걸쭉한 농도가 될 때까지 저어가며 끓인다.
Add the ground pumpkin to a pot, boil over medium-low heat while stirring, and once it comes to a boil, add the water mixed with glutinous rice flour, the kidney beans, and sugar, and continue to boil while stirring until it thickens.

6 냄비의 가운데까지 끓으면 기호에 따라 소금으로 간을 맞추고 완성한다.
When the porridge through to the center of the pot is boiling, complete by salting to taste according to your preferences.

TIPS

* The kidney beans or red bean should be soaked beforehand to shorten the boiling time.

Vocabulary

재료 INGREDIENTS

늙은 호박 [neulgeun hobak]
pumpkin

note
Unlike other squash such as Korean squash, pumpkins are large and orange in color. In Korean food, they are used when making juk (porridge) or tteok.

강낭콩 [gangnangkong]
kidney bean

note
Kidney beans are eaten cooked on top of rice, and are also used as a minor ingredient in tteok or juk.

요리 COOKING

Base Form	Meaning	Examples
짧아지다 [jjalbajida]	to shorten	• 콩을 불리면 삶는 시간이 **짧아져요**. If you soak the beans, the boiling time will be shortened. • 요리 시간이 **짧아지면** 좋겠어요. It's better if the cooking time is shortened.
쉽다 [swiptta]	to be easy	• 전자레인지에 돌리면 자르기 **쉬워요**. If you heat it in the microwave, it will be easy to cut. • 계속 저으면 **쉽게** 녹아요. If you keep stirring, it will dissolve easily.
파내다 [panaeda]	to hollow out	• 호박은 속을 **파내세요**. Hollow out the inside of the pumpkin. • 속을 **파낸** 호박을 찜통에 찌세요. Steam the hollowed out pumpkin in a steamer.

Let's Speak Korean!

🔊 삶기 전에 불리세요.

Track 151

A 콩이 빨리 안 익어요. Beans don't cook quickly.

B 삶기 전에 불리세요. Soak them before you boil them.

"V + −기 전에" is an expression used when indicating an action or state that occurs before another action or state.

Ex 삶(다) + −기 전에 → 삶기 전에
끄(다) + −기 전에 → 끄기 전에

✦ 불을 끄기 전에 파를 넣으세요. Add the green onion before turning off the heat.

✦ 삼계탕을 먹기 전에 소금을 넣으세요. Add salt before eating the samgyetang.

✦ 국물이 끓기 전에 고기를 넣으세요. Add the meat before the soup boils.

🔊 호박부터 잘라 주세요.

Track 152

A 뭘 먼저 할까요? What should I do first?

B 호박부터 잘라 주세요. Cut the pumpkin first.

"N + 부터" is a postpositional particle attached after a noun to indicate the start of a range related to a thing or state. This is frequently followed by 까지, indicating an end.

Ex 호박부터   재료부터   1시부터   어제부터   여기부터

A 뭐부터 넣을까요? What should I add first?

B 고기부터 넣으세요. Add the meat first.

파	닭고기	채소

핫도그
Hot dog

• HOT DOG •

Korean-style hot dogs are a snack made by putting sausage or cheese on wooden skewers, covering in flour batter, and after deep-frying, sprinkling with sugar, ketchup, mustard, etc. In the past, they only contained sausage, but recently, cheese hot dogs made by adding mozzarella cheese instead of sausage are popular. Korean-style hot dogs are a variation of Western-style hot dogs created after they entered Korea and look just like a Western-style hot dog put on a stick, but the way they are made and the taste are different.

재료 INGREDIENTS

2인분 Serves 2

밀가루 250g
250 grams of flour

설탕 30g
30 grams of sugar

소금 4g
4 grams of salt

드라이이스트 6g
6 grams of dry yeast

달걀 1개
1 egg

미지근한 물 1/2컵
1/2 cup of lukewarm water

소시지 3개
3 sausages

스트링치즈 2개 (또는 모차렐
라 치즈)
2 sticks of string cheese (or mozzarella cheese)

빵가루 100g
100 grams of bread crumbs

나무 꼬치 5개
5 wooden skewers

케첩
ketchup

식용유
cooking oil

준비 PREPARATION

◆ 꼬치의 길이에 맞추어 소시지와 치즈의 양을 가감하여 준비한다.
Prepare the amount of sausage and cheese by adding or subtracting to match the length of the skewers.

◆ 밀가루 대신 핫케이크 가루를 사용하면 반죽에 들어가는 설탕, 소금, 드라이이스트는 필요하지 않다.
If hot cake mix is used instead of flour, then the sugar, salt, and dry yeast for the dough are not needed.

요리 COOKING

1 미지근한 물에 드라이이스트를 녹이고, 밀가루를 체에 내린다.
Dissolve the dry yeast in lukewarm water and sift the flour with a sieve.

2 볼에 밀가루, 설탕, 소금, 드라이이스트 녹인 물, 달걀을 넣고 골고루 섞는다.
Add the flour, sugar, salt, water with dissolved dry yeast, and eggs to a bowl and mix evenly.

3 따뜻한 곳에서 반죽이 2배가 될 때까지 발효시킨다.
Ferment the dough in a warm place until it becomes double the size.

4 소시지와 치즈는 꼬치의 길이에 맞추어 잘라 꼬치에 끼우고 밀가루를 입힌다.
Cut the sausage and cheese to match the length of the skewers, put them on the skewers, and dredge in flour.

5 밀가루 입힌 꼬치를 반죽과 빵가루를 순서대로 입혀 섭씨 170도에서 튀긴다.
Dredge the floured skewers in the dough and then in the bread crumbs in that order, then deep-fry at 170 degrees Celsius.

6 튀겨진 핫도그를 기름을 빼고 케첩을 뿌린다. 기호에 따라 설탕, 머스터드를 뿌린다.
Remove the oil from the deep-fried hot dogs and sprinkle with ketchup. According to your preferences, sprinkle with sugar or mustard.

재료 INGREDIENTS

Track 153

빵가루 [ppangkkaru]
bread crumbs

note
Bread crumbs are used when deep-frying fish or meat to increase the crispy texture.

소금 [sogeum]
salt

note
The salt used in Korean food includes ordinary sun-dried salt, seasoned salt, etc. When making kimchi, sun-dried salt, which is created by evaporating sea water via sunlight and wind, is used.

요리 COOKING

Track 154

Base Form	Meaning	Examples
녹이다 [nogida]	to dissolve	• 드라이 이스트를 물에 **녹이세요**. Dissolve the dry yeast in water. • 설탕을 **녹인** 물을 준비하세요. Prepare water with dissolved sugar.
내리다 [naerida]	to sift	• 밀가루를 체에 **내리세요**. Sift the flour with a sieve. • 체에 **내린** 밀가루에 이스트를 넣으세요. Add the yeast to the sifted flour.
되다 [doeda]	to become	• 반죽이 두 배가 **될** 때까지 기다려요. Wait until the dough becomes double the size. • 동그랑땡 모양이 예쁘게 **됐어요**. The shape of the donggeurangttaeng came out nicely/prettily.

Let's Speak Korean!

 소시지나 치즈 있어요?

Track 155

A 소시지나 치즈 있어요? Do you have sausage or cheese?

B 네, 둘 다 있어요. Yes, I have both.

"N + (이)나" is used when expressing that, of two or more objects connected with a similar qualification, only one is chosen.

> Final consonant O + 이나: 호박<u>이나</u>   빵<u>이나</u>   마늘<u>이나</u>
>
> Final consonant X + 나: 김치<u>나</u>   소시지<u>나</u>   파<u>나</u>

Exercise

A **어떤 재료가 필요해요?** What ingredients do you need?

B **김치나 깍두기가 필요해요.** I need kimchi or kkakdugi.

> 양파 / 파   감자 / 고구마   새우젓 / 소금

 요리를 잘해요?

Track 156

A 요리를 잘해요? Can you cook well?

B 아니요, 요리를 못해요. No, I can't cook.

"N + 을/를 잘하다" is an expression indicating that the object indicated by 을/를 can be performed skillfully. The opposite expression is "N + 을/를 못하다."

> Final consonant O + 을 잘해요 / 못해요: 김치찜 + 을 잘해요 / 못해요 →
>
> 김치찜<u>을</u> 잘해요 / 못해요
>
> Final consonant X + 를 잘해요 / 못해요: 된장찌개 + 를 잘해요 / 못해요 →
>
> 된장찌개<u>를</u> 잘해요 / 못해요

Exercise

A **한국 음식을 잘해요?** Can you cook Korean food well?

B **네, 한국 음식을 <u>잘해요</u>.** Yes, I can cook (Korean food) well.

A **축구를 잘해요?** Can you play soccer well?

B **아니요, 축구를 <u>못해요</u>.** No, I can't play soccer.

짜파구리
Jjapaguri

• JJAPAGURI (RAM-DON) •

Jjapaguri, which appeared in the movie "Parasite," is a Korean food
that became famous as the movie grew into a global hit. The Korean name
combines the first 2 characters of "Jjapaghetti," the name of an instant noodle
product, with the last 2 characters of "Neoguri," the name of another product.
The English name, ram-don, combines the first syllable of "ramen" and the
last syllable of "udon." Like its name suggests, jjapaguri is cooked from 2 styles
of noodles and has a very unique taste. And like in the film,
when eaten with striploin on top, a rich taste can be felt.

재료 INGREDIENTS

2인분 Serves 2

짜파게티 라면 1봉
1 package of Jjapaghetti brand instant noodles

너구리 라면 1봉
1 package of Neoguri brand instant noodles

물 500ml
500 milliliters of water

소고기 스테이크용 200g
200 grams of beef for steak

소금 약간
a pinch of salt

후춧가루 조금
a pinch of ground black pepper

준비 PREPARATION

◆ 보통 2인분은 너구리1+짜파게티1, 3인분은 너구리1+짜파게티2 정도 준비한다.
Ordinarily, for 2 people, prepare 1 pack of Neoguri and 1 pack of Jjapaghetti, and for 3 people, prepare 1 pack of Neoguri and 2 packs of Jjapaghetti.

◆ 만드는 방법은 삶은 면에 분말수프를 넣고 볶는 방법과 면을 삶으면서 분말수프를 넣고 한 번에 조리하는 방법이 있다. 여기서는 후자의 방법을 소개한다.
This can be made by adding powdered soup to boiled noodles and stir-frying, or by adding powdered soup while boiling to cook all at once. The latter method is introduced here.

요리 COOKING

1 소고기는 소금과 후춧가루를 뿌려 둔다.
Sprinkle the beef with salt and ground black pepper.

2 냄비에 물이 끓으면 면 2개와 후레이크 2개, 너구리 분말수프 1/2, 다시마를 먼저 넣는다. Boil water in a pot, add two blocks of instant noodles, 2 packets of soup flakes, 1/2 of the Neoguri powdered soup, and kelp first.

3 라면이 끓는 동안 중불에서 소고기를 원하는 정도로 익혀 프라이팬에 그대로 둔다.
While the noodles are boiling, cook the beef to the desired degree over medium heat and leave in the frying pan.

4 라면이 반쯤 익으면 짜파게티의 분말수프와 포장된 오일을 넣고 끓인다.
When the noodles are half cooked, add the Jjapaghetti powdered soup and oil packet, and then boil.

5 수프가 뭉치지 않고 잘 섞이도록 저어 주며 국물이 2큰술 정도 남을 때까지 졸인다.
Stir to mix well so that the powdered soup does not clump, and reduce until about 2 tablespoons of soup are left.

6 국물이 2큰술 정도 남으면 프라이팬에 있는 육즙을 넣고 섞은 후 그릇에 담고 소고기를 얹는다. When 2 tablespoons of soup are left, add the beef gravy from the frying pan and, after mixing, put in a bowl and place the beef on top.

 Tips

* Striploin is the cut of meat that provides the best taste, so prepare a cut used for steak.

Vocabulary

재료 INGREDIENTS

Track 157

채끝 [chaekkeut]
striploin

note

This is the lower part of a cut of sirloin. This cut of beef has little fat.

라면 [ramyeon]
ramyeon

note

When people say "ramyeon," they are usually referring to instant noodles. Because Korean people are accustomed to spice, most ramyeon has a fairly spicy taste. In addition to ramyeon soup, there is jjajang (black bean) ramyeon, bibim (spicy mixed) ramyeon, etc.

요리 COOKING

Track 158

Base Form	Meaning	Examples
조리하다 [jorihada]	to cook	• 제가 **조리하는** 방법과 달라요. My method of cooking is different. • 순서에 따라 **조리해요.** Cook according to the steps in order.
요리하다 [yorihada]	to cook	• 호박과 양파로 무슨 음식을 **요리할까요**? What kind of food should we cook with squash and onion? • 저는 지금 **요리해요.** I'm cooking right now.
남다 [namtta]	to be left	• 고기가 익으면 프라이팬에 **남겨** 두세요. When the meat has cooked, leave it in the frying pan. • 국물이 두 큰술 **남으면** 불을 끄세요. When there are 2 tablespoons of soup left, turn off the heat.

Let's Speak Korean!

○ 3분 더 끓이세요.

Track 159

A 얼마나 더 끓여야 돼요? How much longer does it need to boil?

B 3분 더 끓여야 돼요. It needs to boil for 3 minutes longer.

The 분 in 3분 is a unit for reading time meaning "minutes." When reading ~분, Sino-Korean numbers are used.

1	2	3	4	5	6	7	8	9	10	20	30	+ 분
일	이	삼	사	오	육	칠	팔	구	십	이십	삼십	

Ex 8분 → 팔 분   30분 → 삼십 분   15분 → 십오 분

Exercise

A 몇 분 지났어요? How many minutes have passed?

B 7분 지났어요. 7 minutes have passed.

이십구 분(29분)   사십 분(40분)

○ 열한 시예요.

Track 160

A 몇 시예요? What time is it?

B 11시예요. It is 11 o'clock.

The 시 in 11시 is a unit for reading time meaning 시간 (hours). When reading the number part of 시, native Korean numbers are used.

1	2	3	4	5	6	7	8	9	10	11	12	+ 시
한	두	세	네	다섯	여섯	일곱	여덟	아홉	열	열하나	열두	

Exercise

A 몇 시예요? What time is it?

B 열 시 사십오 분이에요. (10:45) It's 10:45.

여덟 시 육 분(8:06)   열두 시 사십칠 분(12:47)   아홉 시 십오 분(9:15)

APPENDIX

Explanation in Korean

Index

Ingredients / Cooking Vocabulary

한식 조리의 기본

○ 미리 배우는 기본 썰기 p.14

어슷썰기 대파, 당근 등 긴 재료를 써는 방법으로 칼을 옆으로 비스듬하게 사선으로 하여 썬다.

송송 썰기 풋고추나 쪽파 등을 작은 크기로 써는 방법이다. 보통 음식 위에 얹는 고명이나 양념장을 만들 때 송송 썰기 한다.

반달썰기 호박, 감자, 당근 등을 세로로 반 자른 후 일정하게 반달 모양으로 써는 방법이다.

깍뚝썰기 무, 감자 등을 주사위처럼 정육면체 모양으로 써는 방법이다.

나박 썰기 무 등을 가로, 세로가 비슷한 사각형으로 썬 재료를 다시 얇게 써는 방법이다.

편 썰기 마늘 등을 원하는 두께로 고르고 얇게 써는 방법이다.

채썰기 재료를 원하는 길이로 얇게 편을 썬 다음 겹쳐 놓고 일정한 두께로 가늘게 써는 방법이다.

다지기 채를 썬 재료를 가지런히 모아서 다시 작게 써는 방법이다.

○ 먼저 알아두면 유용한 요리 용어 p.15

한소끔 끓이다 국, 찌개 등을 끓일 때 국물이 한번 끓어 오르는 것을 나타내는 말로 국물 요리를 할 때 많이 사용된다.

한 꼬집 소금이나 설탕 등을 엄지와 검지로 집었을 때의 양을 의미하며 아주 적은 양을 넣어야 할 때 사용하는 말이다.

밑간 음식을 만들기 전에 재료에 간이 잘 배어들도록 미리 간장이나 소금 등으로 재워 놓는 것을 말한다.

자작하다 재료가 국물 밖으로 보일 듯 말 듯 할 정도로 국물이 졸아들어 적은 상태를 의미한다.

무르다 단단한 것이 물렁거리는 상태가 되는 것을 의미한다.

익다 고기나 채소, 곡식 등 날것에 뜨거운 열을 가하여 그 성질과 맛이 달라지는 것을 말한다.

재우다 음식의 맛이 들도록 미리 양념을 무치거나 발라서 일정 시간 놔두는 것을 의미한다.

달구다 프라이팬을 불 위에 올려서 뜨겁게 하는 것을 말한다.

지지다 재료를 불에 달군 프라이팬에 기름을 바르고 부쳐서 익히는 것을 말한다.

두르다 프라이팬에 기름을 고르게 바르거나 얹는 것을 말한다.

데치다 채소, 해산물 등을 끓는 물에 넣어 살짝 익히는 것을 의미한다.

삶다 재료를 물에 넣고 끓이는 것을 말한다.

치대다 반죽 따위를 자꾸 문질러서 덩어리가 없이 점성이 생기게 하는 것을 말한다.

버무리다 여러 가지 재료를 한데에 뒤섞는 것을 의미한다.

찌다 채소나 떡 등을 뜨거운 김으로 익히거나 데우는 것을 의미한다.

뜸 들이다 음식을 삶거나 혹은 밥을 할 때, 열을 가한 뒤 한동안 뚜껑을 열지 않고 잠시 그대로 두어 충분히 잘 익게 하는 것을 말한다.

○ 한식 요리의 계량 및 불의 세기 p.16

◆ 계량

✦ **액체류** 계량컵에 가득 채우기

✦ **가루 또는 알갱이류** 가득 담아 윗면을 평평하게 한다. (윗면 깎기)

◆ 불의 세기

강불/센 불 국물 같은 액체류를 끓일 때, 한소끔 끓일 때, 재료를 빠르게 볶을 때 사용한다.

중불 프라이팬을 달궈야 할 때, 볶음이나 조림 등을 할 때 사용한다.

약불 국물의 깊은 맛을 내거나 단단한 재료를 익히는 등 오랫동안 가열해야 할 때, 음식의 모양을 만들 때, 음식의 뜸을 들여야 할 때 사용한다.

○ 한식에 쓰이는 양념 p.17

✦ **간장의 종류에 따른 활용**
  – 국간장: 국, 나물무침 등
  – 양조간장: 조림, 볶음 등
  – 진간장: 불고기, 갈비 등

○ 한국의 대표 김치 p.18

김치는 제일 먼저 떠오르는 한식 메뉴이며, 한국의 전통 발효 음식의 대표이기도 하다. '김치' 하면 보통은 '배추김치'를 떠올리지만,

김치는 배추, 무, 오이 등과 같은 채소를 소금에 절였다가 고춧가루를 비롯한 각종 양념을 넣어 버무린 후 발효시켜 만든 한국 고유의 발효 음식이다. 김치는 다양한 채소를 주재료로 하여 만들 수 있어서, 배추김치, 깍두기, 오이소박이, 열무김치, 총각김치, 갓김치, 나박김치 등 그 종류도 매우 다양하다.

배추김치 보통 '김치'라고 하면 떠올리게 되는 것이 배추김치이다. 통배추를 2등분 또는 4등분하여 소금물에 절인 다음 무채와 각종 양념으로 만든 소를 배춧잎 사이사이에 넣어 만들고 통에 담아 숙성시킨다. 이처럼 배추김치를 잘게 자르지 않고 통으로 만든 것을 '포기김치'라고 하며 저장 기간이 긴 김장은 포기김치의 형태로 만든다.

오이소박이 칼집을 낸 오이를 소금에 절여서 양념한 부추소를 칼집 사이사이에 채워 만든 것으로 주로 봄부터 여름에 만들어 먹는다.

깍두기 무를 주사위 모양으로 깍뚝썰기 하여 소금에 절인 뒤 고춧가루와 각종 양념으로 버무려 담근 김치이다.

총각김치 총각무를 무청까지 같이 사용하는데, 무가 큰 것은 적당한 크기로 길게 잘라 소금에 절여서 각종 양념으로 버무려 담근 김치이다.

○ 한식 요리의 시작, 밥 짓기　　　　　p.19

한국인의 대표 주식이며 한식의 기본인 밥은 마른 쌀을 서너 번 씻고 헹구어 물을 넣고 열을 가하여 익힌 음식이다. 솥(혹은 냄비)에 밥을 할 때에는 물의 양을 조절하는 것뿐만 아니라 불 조절을 잘해야 찰지고 맛있는 밥을 지을 수 있었다. 하지만 전기밥솥이 대중화되면서 물의 양만 맞추면 원하는 맛의 맛있는 밥을 지을 수 있다. 주로 쌀만으로 밥을 짓지만 콩, 팥, 보리 등을 넣어 잡곡밥을 짓기도 한다.

재료 2-3인분 쌀(멥쌀) 2컵, 물 2와 1/4컵

재료 준비

1. 밥을 할 때에 물의 양은 마른 쌀의 경우 쌀 부피의 1.2배(또는 중량의 1.5배)이며, 불린 쌀은 쌀과 물이 1:1의 비율로 물을 붓는다.

2. 전기밥솥을 이용하여 밥을 짓는 경우는 만들기 1-3의 과정을 거친 후 전기밥솥의 사용법에 따라 밥을 하면 된다.

만들기

1. 쌀을 바가지나 큰 그릇에 담고 물을 충분히 부은 뒤 재빨리 섞어서 바로 물을 따라 버리고 힘 있게 비벼 주는 동작을 반복하여 쌀 표면의 불순물을 제거한다. 물이 맑아질 때까지 서너 차례 반복하여 헹군다.

2. 쌀이 충분히 잠길 정도로 물을 붓고 여름에는 30분, 겨울에는 2시간 정도 불린다.

3. 솥(혹은 냄비)에 쌀을 담고 분량의 물을 부어 센 불에서 끓이다가 물이 끓기 시작하면 중불로 줄여 넘치지 않을 정도로 4-5분 끓게 놔 둔다.

4. 불을 중불에서 약불로 줄여 밥물이 잦아들 때까지 10-15분 정도 뜸을 들인다.

5. 불을 끄고 뚜껑을 덮은 채로 5분 두었다가 주걱으로 아래위를 잘 섞어 준다.

한식 레시피

1 김치 Kimchi

김치찌개 Kimchijjigae　　　　　p.22

김치찌개는 잘 익은 신김치로 만든 찌개 요리로, 한식 밥상에 곁들이는 가장 흔한 메뉴 중 하나이며 김치로 만든 대표적인 음식이다. 겨울철 김장 김치가 봄이 되면서 물러지고 신맛이 날 때 찌개로 끓여 먹던 음식으로, 보관 기술이 발달하면서 계절에 관계없이 먹는 음식이 되었다. 돼지고기, 소고기, 멸치, 참치 등 함께 넣은 재료에 따라 다양한 맛을 즐길 수 있다.

> **Let's Speak Korean!**　　　p.25

안녕하세요?

'안녕하세요?'는 누군가를 만났을 때 시간과 관계없이 격식을 차리지 않고 할 수 있는 인사말이다. 이에 비해 '안녕하십니까?'는 정중한 인사말이며, 친구나 아랫사람에게는 '안녕'을 사용할 수 있다.

김치찌개입니다.

'입니다'는 존댓말로 사물, 사람의 이름, 국적 등과 함께 'N + 입니다' 형태로 쓰인다. '입니까?'는 '입니다'의 의문형이다. '이게'는 '이것이'의 줄임말로 'this'의 의미이다.

김치볶음밥 Kimchi-bokkeumbap　　　　　p.26

김치볶음밥은 밥과 잘게 썬 김치 또는 추가로 햄, 소시지 등을 넣고 볶은 밥이다. 김치볶음밥은 한국에 프라이팬이 도입되면서 생겨난 음식이며, 김치와 밥만으로 맛있고 근사한 한 그릇 음식을 만들 수 있다. 김치볶음밥은 김치 종류 중 보통 배추김치를 사용하며, 최근에는 깍두기를 잘게 썰어 만들기도 하며 달걀프라이, 치즈 등을 얹어 먹기도 한다.

Let's Speak Korean! p.29

김치찌개가 아닙니다.

'김치찌개' 뒤에 붙은 '이'는 주격 조사이다. 주격 조사는 앞에 오는 명사가 자음으로 끝나면 '이'를 모음으로 끝나면 '가'를 붙인다. 'N + 이/가 아닙니다'는 'N + 입니다'에 대한 부정의 의미를 나타낸다.

그게 김치입니다.

'이게', '그게', '저게'는 '이것이', '그것이', '저것이'의 줄임말로 '이것', '그것', '저것'에 주격 조사 '이'가 붙은 것이다. '이것'은 화자에게 가까운 사물을, '그것'은 청자에게 가까운 사물을, '저것'은 화자와 청자 모두에게서 멀리 있는 사물을 가리킬 때 쓰인다.

김치전 Kimchijeon p.30

김치전은 밀기루 반죽에 김치를 송송 썰어 넣고 프라이팬에 지글지글 부친 전의 한 종류이다. 김치찌개, 김치볶음밥과 함께 김치를 활용한 대표적인 음식이다. 간식으로 많이 먹으며 반찬이나 술안주로도 즐겨 먹는다. 오징어, 새우 같은 해산물이나 햄, 소시지 등 김치와 잘 어울리는 재료를 더 넣으면 특별한 김치전을 만들 수 있다.

Let's Speak Korean! p.33

밀가루예요.

'예요'는 to be와 같은 뜻이며 반드시 끝음절이 모음으로 끝나는 명사 뒤에 붙여서 쓴다. '예요' 뒤에 물음표(?)를 붙이면 의문문, 온점(.)을 붙이면 평서문이 된다.

김치전이에요.

'이에요'는 '예요'처럼 'to be'의 뜻이며 반드시 끝음절이 자음으로 끝나는 명사 뒤에 붙여서 쓴다. '이에요' 뒤에 물음표(?)를 붙이면 의문문, 온점(.)을 붙이면 평서문이 된다.

김치찜 Kimchijjim p.34

김치찜은 묵은지 또는 신 김치에 두툼한 돼지고기를 넣고 국물을 자작하게 조려 익힌 찜 요리이다. 약불에서 오랫동안 끓이기 때문에 김치와 돼지고기가 매우 부드러우며 두 재료가 어우러진 국물맛도 일품이다. 재료는 돼지고기 김치찌개와 거의 같지만 김치찌개보다 돼지고기가 더 많이 들어가서 주요리에 속한다.

Let's Speak Korean! p.37

이 음식은 김치찜이에요.

'은/는'은 화제를 나타내는 말 뒤에 붙는 조사이다. 앞에 오는 말이 자음으로 끝나면 '은', 모음으로 끝나면 '는'을 사용한다.

오늘 메뉴가 뭐예요?

'뭐예요?'에서 '뭐'는 'what'의 의미로 '뭐예요?'는 'What is'의 의미가 된다.

배추김치 Baechukimchi p.38

배추를 소금에 절여 고춧가루, 무채, 파, 마늘, 젓갈 등으로 소를 만들어 배추 사이에 채워 넣기도 하고, 절인 배추에 고춧가루, 파, 마늘 젓갈 등의 양념을 넣고 버무리기도 하여 발효시킨 음식이다. 배추김치는 한식의 대표적인 음식으로 한식 상차림의 기본 반찬이다. 한국에는 추운 겨울이 오기 전 많은 양의 김치를 담가 보관하던 '김장' 문화가 있다.

Let's Speak Korean! p.43

요리해요.

'해요'는 동사 '하다'의 활용형으로 어미 '-여요'가 붙은 형태이며, '해요?'는 의문형이다. '해요'는 단독으로 쓰일 수도 있고, 'N + 해요'의 형태로 일부 명사와 결합하여 동사로 쓰인다.

언제 해요?

'언제'는 시간을 묻는 의문사이며, '언제 해요?'에 대한 대답은 '언제' 자리에 시간을 나타내는 말을 넣으면 된다.

2 쌀 Rice

떡꼬치 Tteok-kkochi p.44

떡꼬치는 떡볶이떡을 꼬치에 나란히 끼워서 튀기거나 프라이팬에 기름을 넉넉히 넣고 구워서 소스를 발라 먹는 음식이다. 떡볶이와는 다르게 겉은 바삭하고 속은 쫄깃하다. 기름에 튀기거나 구웠기 때문에 고소하면서도 고추장과 케첩을 섞은 소스 때문에 매콤한 맛과 새콤달콤한 맛을 동시에 느낄 수 있다. 떡볶이와 함께 길거리 음식으로도 유명하며 요즘은 집에서도 간식으로 많이 만들어 먹는다.

Let's Speak Korean! p.47

떡볶이하고 달라요.

'N + 하고 다르다'의 '하고'는 다른 것과 비교하거나 기준으로 삼는 대상임을 나타내는 조사이다. 'N₁ + 하고 N₂'와 다른 의미이다.

정말 맛있네요.

'-네요'는 생각이나 느낌의 감탄을 나타내는 종결 어미이다. 'V/A + -네요'의 형태로 활용한다.

떡볶이 Tteokbokki p.48

떡볶이는 가래떡을 한입 크기로 썰거나 떡볶이떡으로 만들어진 것을 고추장, 어묵 등과 함께 끓여 먹는 매콤한 음식이다. 쫄깃한 떡에 매콤하면서도 달달한 국물을 듬뿍 찍어 먹으면 더욱 맛있다. 떡볶이는 대표적인 길거리 음식이기도 한데, 함께 파는 튀김이나 순대를 함께 먹어도 잘 어울린다. 떡볶이떡은 쌀떡과 밀떡이 있으며 기호에 따라 선택하면 된다.

> **Let's Speak Korean!** p.51

고추장을 넣었어요.
'–았/었–'은 어떤 동작이나 상태가 끝난 상태를 나타내는 과거 시제 선어말 어미이다.

고추장 때문에 매워요.
'때문에'는 'N + 때문에'의 형태로 사람이나 사물이 어떤 일의 원인이나 까닭임을 나타낼 때 쓰인다.

궁중떡볶이 Gungjungtteokbokki p.52

가래떡을 한 입 크기 정도로 썰어 소고기, 표고버섯 등을 넣고 간장, 참기름으로 양념하여 볶은 음식이다. 예부터 궁중에서 즐겨 먹었기 때문에 궁중떡볶이라고 하며 고추장이 아닌 간장을 사용하여 간장떡볶이라고도 한다. 맵지 않고 간장에 볶은 떡, 소고기, 버섯의 맛이 조화를 이룬다. 최근에는 파프리카, 당근 등을 같이 넣어 보는 즐거움을 높이기도 한다.

> **Let's Speak Korean!** p.55

짜요? 싱거워요?
'짜다', '싱겁다'는 맛을 표현하는 단어이다. 이 외에도 맛을 나타내는 단어로는 '맵다', '달다' 등이 있다.

이건 맵지 않아요.
'–지 않다'는 어떤 행동이나 상황을 부정할 때 사용되며, '안'과 같은 의미이다.

비빔밥 Bibimbap p.56

비빔밥은 밥 위에 각종 나물과 고기를 올리고 고추장이나 간장을 넣어 비벼 먹는 음식이다. 예전에는 '비빔밥' 대신 '어지럽게 섞는다'는 의미의 '골동반'이라고 불렸다. 비빔밥은 한식을 대표하는 메뉴이며 한국인은 외국인들에게도 인기가 많다. 나물을 만들기 어려운 경우는 밥에 나물 대신 각종 볶은 채소와 고추장을 넣어 비벼 먹기도 한다.

> **Let's Speak Korean!** p.59

가끔 먹어요.
'자주', '가끔'은 어떤 현상이나 일이 반복되는 정도를 나타내는 부

사이다. 빈번한 정도에 따라 다음과 같은 단어를 사용할 수 있다.

비빔밥을 먹어 봤어요?
'아/어 보다'는 시도했거나 경험했던 행동에 대해 말할 때 사용하는 표현이다.

김밥 Gimbap p.60

김밥은 김 위에 밥을 얇게 펴고 그 위에 단무지, 달걀, 당근을 비롯하여 햄, 어묵, 다양한 채소들을 넣고 말아서 먹는 음식이다. 김밥은 간편하게 먹을 수 있어서 소풍이나 여행을 갈 때 또는 도시락 메뉴로 유명하다. 속 재료에 따라 참치 김밥, 김치 김밥, 달걀 김밥, 치즈 김밥 등이 있으며 색색의 여러 가지 재료가 어우러져 보는 즐거움을 더해 준다.

> **Let's Speak Korean!** p.64

집에서 먹었어요.
'에서'는 행동이 이루어지고 있는 장소를 나타내는 조사이다. 'N + 에서'의 형태로 장소를 나타내는 명사에 붙여 쓴다.

김밥로 말아 보세요.
'–아/어 보세요'는 다른 사람에게 어떤 일을 해 보도록 권유할 때 사용하는 표현이다.

3 달걀·두부 Eggs·Tofu

달걀말이 Dalgyalmari p.65

달걀을 푼 물을 그대로 또는 송송 썬 파 등의 채소를 넣고 팬에서 익히면서 둥글게 만 음식이다. 달걀 푼 물을 말아서 만들었기 때문에 '달걀말이'라고 하며 '계란말이'라고도 한다. 파 외에도 당근, 양파 등 다진 채소와 햄, 소시지, 치즈 등을 넣어 다양하게 응용이 가능하며, 도시락 반찬으로 많이 활용된다.

> **Let's Speak Korean!** p.67

누가 만들었어요?
'누가'는 '누구 + 가'의 줄임 형태이며, '누구'는 'who', '가'는 주격 조사이다. '지수 씨'는 사람의 이름에 '씨'를 붙여 그 사람을 높여 부르는 말이다. 질문 받은 사람이 본인이 주체가 되어 답하는 때는 자신을 낮추어 상대방을 높이는 '제가'를 사용한다.

달걀말이를 만들까요?
'V + –(으)ㄹ까요?'는 어떤 일에 대하여 상대방의 의사를 묻는 종결 어미이다.

계란찜 Gyeranjjim　　　　p.68

계란찜은 새우젓이나 소금으로 간을 하여 직화 또는 중탕으로 쩌 낸 음식이다. 달걀물에 당근, 양파, 대파 등을 넣어 예쁜 색깔의 달 걀찜을 만들 수 있다. 계란찜은 부드럽고 자극적이지 않아 아이들 한테도 인기가 있는 반찬이며, 매운 음식과도 잘 어울린다. 요즘은 뚝배기를 사용하여 직화로 익히는 방법이 인기가 있는데 이것을 '폭탄 계란찜'이라고 한다.

Let's Speak Korean!　　　　p.71

기다려야 돼요.
동사 뒤에 '-아/어야 돼요'를 붙이면 어떤 행동이나 상황의 필요성 을 나타낸다. 'V+-아/어야 돼요?'는 의문형이다.

대파를 넣고 섞으세요.
'-고'는 어떤 일의 행동을 순서에 따라 연결하는 어미이다. 'V₁+고 V₂'의 형태로 V₁이 V₂보다 먼저 행해진다.

두부부침 Dububuchim　　　　p.72

두부를 들기름에 노릇노릇하게 지져서 참기름, 깨소금을 넣은 간 장에 찍어 먹는 음식이다. 들기름 두부부침은 들기름의 풍미와 두 부의 고소함을, 달걀 두부부침은 부드러움과 고소함을 즐길 수 있 다. 두부는 예부터 서민들이 단백질 섭취를 위해 즐겨 먹던 식재료 이며, 두부부침은 명절에 만드는 전의 한 종류이지만 평소에도 쉽 게 만들어 먹는다.

Let's Speak Korean!　　　　p.75

뒤집어도 돼요?
'V+-아/어도 돼요?'는 어떤 동작에 대해 다른 사람의 동의를 얻 을 때 사용한다. 긍정 대답은 'V+-아/어도 돼요', 부정 대답은 '안 돼요'를 사용한다.

뜨거우니까 조심하세요.
'V+-(으)니까'는 앞의 절이 뒤에 나오는 절의 원인이나 근거가 됨 을 나타낼 때 사용하는 연결 어미이다.

두부김치 Dubukimchi　　　　p.76

두부김치는 따뜻한 두부에 기름에 볶은 김치를 곁들인 음식이다. 두부와 볶은 김치를 함께 먹으면 두부의 부드럽고 고소한 맛과 김 치의 깊은 맛과 아삭한 식감이 어우러져 입을 즐겁게 한다. 뽀얀 두부와 발그스름한 김치는 보는 것만으로도 식욕을 자극한다. 두 부김치는 한국 술 막걸리나 소주와도 잘 어울려 안주로도 인기가 많다.

Let's Speak Korean!　　　　p.79

김치를 볶아 주세요.
'V+-아/어 주다'는 다른 사람을 위해 어떤 동작을 함을 나타내는 표현이다. 주로 다른 사람에게 무언가를 제안하거나 약속할 때, 다 른 사람에게 부탁할 때 사용한다.

김치가 조금 매워요.
'맵다'가 모음으로 시작하는 어미 '-어요'과 결합할 때 어간의 받침 'ㅂ'이 '우'로 바뀌는데, 이를 'ㅂ불규칙'이라고 한다. '굽다', '아름답 다' 등이 이에 해당한다.

순두부찌개 Sundubujjigae　　　　p.80

순두부에 돼지고기, 소고기, 조개류 등과 고춧가루를 넣고 바글바 글 끓인 음식이다. 매콤하면서도 시원한 국물이 식욕을 자극하고 부드러운 두부가 매운 입을 달래 주는 조화로움이 가득한 음식이 다. 뚝배기에 끓여 달걀을 얹은 순두부찌개는 보글보글 끓고 있는 모습과 소리만으로도 군침이 돌게 한다.

Let's Speak Korean!　　　　p.83

못 먹어 봤어요
'못'은 동사가 나타내는 동작을 할 수 없거나 상태가 이루어지지 않았다는 부정의 의미를 나타낸다. '못'은 동사 앞에 사용한다.

조개를 사용한다면 지금 넣으세요.
'-ㄴ다면'은 어떤 동작을 할 것이라고 예상되는 말을 가정하여 조 건으로 삼음을 나타내는 말이다.

4 고기 Meat

불고기 Bulgogi　　　　p.84

불고기는 얇게 썬 소고기를 간장과 갖은 양념에 재워 두었다가 구 워 먹는 음식이다. 불고기 양념은 간장에 단맛을 내는 배나 설탕 을 기본으로 하고 있어서 달달하면서도 짭조름한 맛이 누구에게 나 매력적이다. 불고기라는 이름은 고기를 불에 굽는다는 의미로 예전에는 재워 둔 고기를 석쇠에 놓고 구워 먹었다. 그러나 요즘은 프라이팬에 볶듯이 익혀서 먹는 것이 일반적이다.

Let's Speak Korean!　　　　p.87

소고기 있어요?
'있어요?'는 어떤 사물이 존재한다는 의미인 '있다'의 활용형으로 사물의 존재 여부를 물어볼 때 사용한다. 보통 'N(이/가) 있어요?'

의 형태로 쓰이며, 질문에 대한 긍정 대답은 '네, 있어요.'를 사용한다.

아니요, 없어요.

'없어요'는 '없다'의 활용형이며 '있다'와 반대되는 의미를 가진다. 'N 있어요?'라는 질문에 대한 부정의 대답으로 '(N) 없어요.'를 사용한다. '있다/없다'의 활용은 물건을 살 때, 식당에서 주문할 때도 활용된다.

갈비탕 Galbitang   p.88

갈비탕은 소갈비를 물을 넣고 은근한 불에 갈비에 붙은 살들이 부드럽게 떨어질 만큼 오랫동안 끓여서 먹는 국물 음식이다. 오래 끓여서 잘 무른 고기는 뼈를 들고 뜯어 먹고, 깊고 진한 국물에 흰 쌀밥을 말아서 깍두기와 함께 먹으면 가장 맛있다. 소갈비는 예나 지금이나 비싼 식재료이지만, 갈비탕 한 그릇은 속을 든든하게 채우고 보양할 수 있는 음식이다.

Let's Speak Korean!   p.91

어디 있어요?

'어디'는 'N 어디 있어요?'로 쓰여 사물이나 사람의 소재나 행방을 물을 때 사용한다. 이에 대한 대답으로 '여기/거기/저기 있어요.'를 사용할 수 있으며, '여기'는 화자에게, '거기'는 청자에게 가까운 곳을 가리키며, '저기'는 화자와 청자 모두에게 멀리 있는 곳을 가리킨다.

식탁 위에 있어요.

'어디 있어요?'에 대해 구체적인 위치를 설명해야 할 때에는 '위/아래/안/밖 + 에 있어요.'의 형태로 대답할 수 있다. '위/아래/안/밖'은 반드시 '에'를 붙여야 한다.

갈비구이 Galbigui   p.92

갈비구이는 소갈비에서 살을 얇게 발라 펼쳐서 간장을 기본으로 한 양념에 재웠다가 숯불에 구운 음식이다. 불고기와 양념이 거의 같지만, 고기의 부위가 다르기 때문에 식감과 맛이 차이가 있다. 숯불에 구우면 숯불의 향이 고기에 배어들어 맛을 더해 주며, 프라이팬에 구우면 양념이 끝까지 배어들어 달달하고 짭조름한 맛이 더욱 깊어진다.

Let's Speak Korean!   p.95

갈비구이 만들어요.

'-아/어요'는 현재 시제를 나타내는 비격식체의 높임의 종결 어미이다. 이미 잘 알고 있는 친숙한 사람에게 말할 때 쓰인다.

점심을 먹어요.

'을/를'은 목적격 조사로 앞에 있는 명사가 목적어임을 나타낸다.

갈비찜 Galbijjim   p.96

갈비찜은 소갈비 또는 돼지갈비와 무, 당근, 표고버섯 등을 간장으로 양념하여 은근히 끓여 부드럽게 만든 음식이다. 갈비 특히 소갈비는 한우 중에서 가장 비싼 부위이며 소의 갈비에서 발라낸 고기는 특별한 맛을 가지고 있어서 갈비찜은 맛있고 고급스러운 음식의 대표라고 할 수 있다. 따라서 갈비찜은 명절이나 생일날, 특별한 날에 먹는 음식으로 여겨지고 있다.

Let's Speak Korean!   p.99

불을 줄이세요.

'-(으)세요'는 동사의 어간 뒤에 붙어서 다른 사람에게 어떤 동작을 행하도록 요구하거나 지시할 때 사용할 수 있다.

얼마나 넣어요?

'얼마'는 의문문에 쓰여 수량이나 정도를 물어볼 때 쓰는 말이며, '얼마나'의 '나'는 '얼마'의 뜻을 강조하거나 더해 주는 역할을 한다. '다섯 컵'의 '컵'은 단위를 나타내는 말로 사용되었으며, '숫자 + 단위 명사'로 사용한다.

장조림 Jangjorim   p.100

장조림은 소고기나 돼지고기를 큼직하게 토막 내어 간장과 설탕을 넣고 조린 밑반찬이다. 큼직한 고기를 결대로 잘게 찢어서 간장과 함께 반찬으로 상에 올리는데, 고기 육수와 간장, 설탕이 조려지면서 조화로운 감칠맛을 내기 때문에 밥 한 그릇을 순식간에 비워 버리게 된다.

Let's Speak Korean!   p103

마늘요.

'N + 요'는 질문에 대해 간단히 대답할 때 사용할 수 있다. '마늘요'는 '마늘이 필요해요'를 핵심만 간단히 줄여서 표현한 것이다.

몇 개 필요해요?

'몇'은 수를 물을 때 쓰는 말이다. '개'는 물건을 세는 단위이다. 따라서 물건의 개수를 물을 때 '몇 개 ~ ?'의 표현을 사용하면 된다.

소고기뭇국 Sogogi-mutguk   p.104

소고기뭇국은 소고기로 국물을 내고 여기에 무를 넣고 끓인 국이다. 사계절 언제나 먹을 수 있지만 특히 겨울에는 무가 단맛을 내기 때문에 겨울에 끓여 먹는 소고기뭇국은 더 깊은 감칠맛을 낸다. 자극적이지 않아 어린이들도 먹을 수 있으며 한국 사람들은 일상적으로 많이 먹는 국이다.

Let's Speak Korean!　　　　p.107

안 매워요.
'안'은 부정의 의미를 나타내는 부정 부사로 동사나 형용사의 앞에 쓰인다.

국물만 더 주세요.
'만'은 명사 뒤에 붙어서 어떤 것을 한정하는 의미는 나타낼 때 사용된다. '더'는 어떤 기준 이상의 의미이다.

고추장불고기 Gochujangbulgogi　　　　p.108

돼지고기를 얇게 썰어 고추장을 비롯한 갖은 양념에 재웠다가 구워 먹는 음식이다. 고추장이 돼지고기 특유의 냄새를 없애 주고, 볶을 때 나오는 지방과 어우러져 육질을 부드럽게 만들어 준다. 재워둔 고기를 중불에서 달달 볶으면 고추장 양념이 자극적이지 않으면서 자꾸 끌리는 매력적이 매콤한 맛이 난다.

Let's Speak Korean!　　　　p.111

고추장불고기 어때요?
'어때요?'는 다른 사람에게 어떤 것을 제안하거나 상대방의 의사를 물을 때 사용한다. 보통 명사 뒤에 조사가 생략된 'N 어때요?'의 형태로 사용한다.

맵지만 맛있어요.
'–지만'은 앞의 내용을 긍정하면서 뒤에 그에 반대되는 내용을 말할 때 쓰는 연결 어미이다. 따라서 '–지만' 앞과 뒤의 내용은 상반되며, 동사 어간에 '–지만'을 붙여 쓴다.

동그랑땡 Donggeurangttaeng　　　　p.112

동그랑땡은 간 돼지고기나 소고기를 두부, 다진 채소와 섞어 동글납작하게 모양을 만들어 달걀옷을 입혀서 지진 전의 한 종류이다. 동그란 모양 때문에 육원전, 완자전이라고도 한다. 따뜻할 때 먹는 동그랑땡은 육즙이 가득하고 채소와 두부가 어우러져 느끼하지 않다. 보통 반찬이나 술안주로 먹으며, 명절날이나 생일날 많이 만드는 전의 한 종류이다.

Let's Speak Korean!　　　　p.115

동그랗게 만들어요.
'–게'는 형용사의 어간 뒤에 붙어 부사처럼 사용될 수 있게 하는 연결 어미로 뒤에 오는 동사를 수식한다.

불고기를 먹고 싶어요.
'–고 싶어요'는 어떤 일을 하고 싶다는 뜻을 표현할 때 사용한다. 동사 뒤에 '–고'를 붙여서 'V+–고 싶다'의 형태로 사용한다.

삼계탕 Samgyetang　　　　p.116

어린 닭의 배 속에 찹쌀, 인삼, 마늘, 대추를 채워 넣고 푹 삶아 만든 음식으로, 한국에서는 땀을 많이 흘리는 여름에 부족 되기 쉬운 영양을 보충하기 위해 많이 먹는 음식이다. 단백질을 비롯하여 몸에 좋은 영양소가 들어있기 때문에 보양식으로 여겨진다. 인삼을 빼기도 하는데 맛에는 크게 차이가 없고, 영양을 높이기 위해 전복을 넣기도 한다.

Let's Speak Korean!　　　　p.119

한 마리 필요해요.
'마리'는 동물이나 물고기를 세는 단위 명사로 '숫자＋마리'의 형태로 활용한다. '한'은 'one'의 의미이며, 단위 명사와 결합되면 '하나'가 '한'으로 바뀐다.

닭고기지요?
'(이)지요?'는 이미 알고 있는 사실을 확인할 때 사용하며, 'N＋(이)지요?'의 형태로 활용하며, 동사/형용사와도 결합하여 쓸 수 있다.

찜닭 Jjimdak　　　　p.120

찜닭은 토막 낸 닭과 감자, 당근 등 각종 채소를 간장 양념을 넣고 끓이다가 당면을 넣어 조려 낸 음식이다. 닭고기가 채소들에서 우러난 국물에 푹 익고 간장 양념에 조려지면서 맛있어지며, 마지막에 넣은 당면은 간장 양념과 잘 어울려 잡채와 같은 느낌이 들기도 한다.

Let's Speak Korean!　　　　p.123

무슨 음식 좋아해요?
'무슨'은 일이나 대상, 물건 등에 대해 물을 때 사용하며, '무슨＋N'의 형태로 사용한다. '무슨＋N ～?'에 대한 대답은 간단히 'N＋요'로 할 수 있다. '다'는 'all'의 의미의 부사로 동사나 형용사 앞에 쓸 수 있다.

닭고기도 좋아해요?
'도'는 명사 뒤에 붙어서 'too', 'also'의 의미를 나타내며, 한 가지를 말하고 다른 하나를 더 보태서 이야기할 때 쓰인다.

닭갈비 Dakgalbi　　　　p.124

닭갈비는 닭다리살이나 토막 낸 닭고기를 고추장 양념에 재웠다가 양배추, 당근 등 채소와 함께 프라이팬에 볶은 음식이다. 춘천의 한 선술집에서 돼지갈비 대신 닭고기를 재워서 구워 팔면서 시작되어 '춘천 닭갈비'라고도 한다. 닭갈비에 떡볶이떡, 고구마 등을 넣어 볶기도 하고 모차렐라 치즈를 얹기도 한다. 닭고기를 다 먹고 남은 양념에 밥을 볶아도 맛있다.

Let's Speak Korean!   p.127

고추장하고 고춧가루도 필요해요.

'하고'는 사람이나 사물을 나열할 때 쓰이는 조사이며, 명사 뒤에
붙여 쓴다.

마늘과 참기름도 필요해요.

'와/과'는 '하고'처럼 사람이나 사물을 나열할 때 쓰이는 조사이며,
명사 뒤에 붙여 쓴다.

5 해산물 Seafood

해물파전 Haemulpajeon   p.128

해물파전은 밀가루 반죽을 입힌 파를 듬뿍 깔고 각종 해산물을 얹
어 노릇하게 지져 낸 음식이다. 파전은 막걸리와 환상의 궁합을
이루는 음식으로 막걸리를 즐기는 사람이 많아지면서 파전도 인
기가 높아지고 있다. 파전의 가장자리는 바삭하고 고소하여 가장
자리를 먼저 먹으려고도 하며, 파전을 직접 만들면 노릇하게 익어
가는 동안 군침이 돌기도 한다.

Let's Speak Korean!   p.131

비가 올 때 해물파전을 만들어요.

'-(으)ㄹ 때'는 어떤 동작이나 현상이 일어나는 시간이라는 의미를
나타낼 때 사용하는 표현이다.

음식을 만드는 중이에요.

'V +-는 중이다'는 무엇을 하는 중간에 있음을 나타내는 표현이
다.

미역국 Miyeokguk   p.132

미역국은 마른 미역을 불려서 은근한 불에서 끓이는 국물 음식이
다. 미역은 미끌미끌한 식감 때문에 싫어하는 사람도 있지만, 미역
국은 깊은 맛의 국물을 위주로 즐기기 때문에 미역의 식감을 싫어
하는 사람도 도전해 볼 만하다. 한국 문화에 있어서 '미역국'은 생
일에 먹는 대표적인 음식이며, 아이를 낳은 산모의 회복을 돕는 음
식으로 알려져 있다.

Let's Speak Korean!   p.135

10월 5일이에요.

'며칠'은 날짜를 물을 때 사용한다. 한국어 고유어와 한자어의 두
가지 숫자 체계가 있으며 날짜를 읽을 때에는 한자어 숫자로 읽는
다.

미역국을 먹었겠어요.

'-겠-'은 어떤 상황에 대한 추측을 나타낼 때 쓰이는 선어말 어미
로 동사/형용사의 어간과 어미 사이에 결합한다.

새우전 Saeujeon   p.136

고기, 생선, 채소 등을 밀가루와 달걀옷을 입혀서 기름을 두른 팬
에 지져내는 음식을 '전'이라고 한다. 새우전도 '전'의 한 종류로 새
우를 통으로 또는 다져서 각종 다진 채소를 넣고 섞어 밀가루와
달걀옷을 입혀 팬에 지진 음식이다. 노릇하게 부친 새우전은 탱글
탱글한 식감이 살아 있어서 씹는 즐거움이 있다. 새우전은 반찬으
로 또는 안주로 먹는다.

Let's Speak Korean!   p.139

삼백 그램 필요해요.

가격, 중량을 말할 때에는 한자어 숫자 체계를 사용한다.

전을 먹어 본 적이 있어요?

'-(으)ㄴ 적이 있다'는 동사와 결합하여 경험을 나타낼 때에 쓰이
는 표현이다. 이에 대한 대답은 간단히 '네, 있어요.' 또는 '아니요,
없어요.'로 할 수 있다.

어묵탕 Eomuktang   p.140

어묵은 생선의 살을 으깨어 소금 등을 넣고 반죽하여 튀긴 것이다.
이렇게 만들어진 다양한 종류의 어묵을 꼬치에 끼워 물을 넉넉히
넣고 무, 양파, 멸치 등과 함께 끓여서 먹는 음식이 어묵탕이다. 추
운 겨울이면 뜨끈한 어묵탕이 생각나고 어묵탕의 국물만 봐도 몸
이 녹는 듯하다. 어묵 꼬치는 떡볶이와 함께 대표적인 길거리 음식
이며 자극적이지 않아 누구나 좋아하는 음식이다.

Let's Speak Korean!   p.143

어떤 계절을 좋아해요?

'어떤'은 사람이나 사물의 특성, 내용, 상태 등에 대해 물을 때 사용
하며, '어떤 + N'의 형태로 사용한다. '어떤 + N ~?'에 대한 대답은
간단히 'N + 요'로 할 수 있다. 계절을 나타내는 말은 봄, 여름, 가
을, 겨울이 있다.

따뜻한 어묵탕요.

'-(으)ㄴ'은 형용사가 뒤에 오는 명사를 꾸밀 수 있게 만들어 주는
어미이다.

오징어볶음 Ojingeo-bokkeum   p.144

오징어볶음은 깨끗하게 손질한 오징어와 양파, 당근 등 채소들을
고추장과 고춧가루 양념에 볶아낸 음식이다. 고추장과 고춧가루
를 기본양념으로 사용하고 여기에 청양고추를 추가로 넣어 만드

는 매운 음식 중 하나이다. 오징어볶음은 반찬으로 먹기도 하지만 밥 위에 얹어 한 그릇 음식으로 밥과 비벼 먹기도 한다. 한국 사람들은 입맛이 없을 때 이런 종류의 매운 음식을 즐기기도 한다.

Let's Speak Korean!   p.147

오징어를 더 좋아해요.
'보다'는 비교의 대상이 되는 말에 붙어 두 대상을 비교할 때 쓰인다. '더'는 'more'의 의미로 뜻을 더해준다.

맛있게 드세요.
'드세요'는 '먹다'의 높임말로 상대방에게 음식 따위를 먹어 보라고 권할 때 사용한다. '맛있게 드세요'는 식사 전에 하는 인사말로도 흔히 쓰인다.

6 기타 Other

된장찌개 Doenjangjjigae   p.148
된장은 콩을 삶아 발효시켜 간장을 담근 후 남은 건더기로 만든 것이다. 된장찌개는 된장을 물에 풀고 호박, 양파 등의 채소와 고기, 두부 등을 함께 넣어 끓인 국물 음식이다. 된장찌개에 들어가는 재료는 따로 정해져 있지 않으며 된장만 있으면 어떤 재료를 조합해도 맛있는 된장찌개가 만들어진다. 된장찌개는 한국 사람들에게 있어서는 '집밥'을 생각나게 하는 음식이며, 한식을 대표하는 음식이기도 하다.

Let's Speak Korean!   p.151

10분쯤 걸려요.
'쯤'은 대략 그만한 정도라는 의미를 더해주는 말이다. '10분'의 '분'은 시간을 읽는 단위이다

된장찌개를 끓이고 있어요.
'-고 있다'는 어떤 일이 진행 중에 있음을 나타내는 표현이다. 'V+-고 있다'의 형태를 활용하며 '-(으)ㄴ 중이다'와 같은 의미이다.

부대찌개 Budaejjigae   p.152
부대찌개는 전골 냄비에 김치와 소시지, 햄 그리고 각종 채소를 담아 육수를 붓고 양념장을 넣어 끓이는 음식이다. 재료에서 이미 알 수 있듯이 부대찌개는 한국의 전통 음식이 아니라 한국 전쟁 때 미군 부대를 통해 소시지와 햄이 전해지면서 생겨난 음식이다. 부대찌개는 김치와 소시지, 햄이 묘한 조화를 이루어 칼칼하면서도 육류에서 우러난 진한 국물 맛을 느낄 수 있다.

Let's Speak Korean!   p.155

물을 많이 넣으면 안 돼요.
'-(으)면 안 되다'는 어떤 행동이 금지되었거나 제한되었음을 나타낸다.

국물이 끓으면 파를 넣으세요.
'-(으)면'은 뒤에 오는 내용에 대한 조건이나 가정을 나타낼 때 사용하는 어미이다.

잡채 Japchae   p.156
삶은 당면과 시금치, 당근, 양파 등 볶은 채소, 고기 등을 간장 양념으로 버무려 먹는 음식이다. 재료들을 각각 양념하여 익힌 후 섞어서 버무리기 때문에 각각의 재료들의 식감이 살아 있으면서도 당면과 채소들의 맛이 어우러진다. 잡채는 예부터 화려하면서도 품격이 있는 음식으로 여겨졌기 때문에 생일잔치, 결혼 피로연 등 각종 잔칫상에 빼놓을 수 없는 음식이다.

Let's Speak Korean!   p.159

생일 파티를 할 거예요.
'-(으)ㄹ 거예요'는 미래에 일어날 사건이나 행동을 나타낼 때 사용하는 표현이다.

식은 후에 넣으세요.
'V+-(으)ㄴ 후에'는 어떤 일 다음에 다른 행동이 뒤따를 때 사용하는 표현이다.

김말이 Gimmari   p.160
김말이는 튀김의 한 종류인데, 당면과 여러 가지 채소들을 김으로 말아 반죽을 입혀 튀긴 음식이다. 김말이는 떡볶이, 어묵 꼬치와 함께 길거리 포장마차나 분식집에서 쉽게 먹을 수 있는 간식이며, 김말이만 먹기 보다는 떡볶이 국물을 찍어 먹으면 그 맛이 일품이다. 집에서는 잡채가 남는 경우 잡채를 그대로 김에 말아서 쉽게 만들 수 있어 떡볶이와 함께 많이 만들어 먹는다.

Let's Speak Korean!   p.163

버리지 마세요.
'V+-지 말다'는 어떤 행동을 하지 못하게 하거나 그만두게 함을 나타낼 때 사용하는 표현이다.

떡볶이하고 같이 드세요.
'같이'는 둘 이상의 사람이나 사물이 함께하다는 의미로 동사 앞에 쓴다. '드세요'는 '먹다(먹어요)'에 대한 높임의 표현이다.

호떡 Hotteok p.164

호떡은 밀가루 반죽을 발효시켜 흑설탕과 견과류로 만든 소를 넣어 기름을 넉넉하게 두른 팬에 구워 내는 간식의 한 종류이다. 겉이 노릇하고 바삭하게 익은 호떡을 한입 베어 물면 초콜릿 혹은 캐러멜 같은 흑설탕 잼이 달콤하게 입 안 가득 퍼진다. 호떡은 길거리 간식 중 하나이며 겨울에 인기가 더 많다. 요즘은 씨앗 호떡, 녹차 호떡 등 이색적인 호떡이 많아졌다.

Let's Speak Korean! p.167

흑설탕과 견과류로 만들어요.
'(으)로'는 어떤 물건의 재료나 원료를 나타낼 때 사용하는 조사로 명사 뒤에 붙여 쓴다.

집에서 만들 수 있어요.
'-(으)ㄹ 수 있어요'는 어떤 일을 할 수 있음을 나타내는 표현이다.

감자전 Gamjajeon p.168

감자전은 생감자를 강판에 곱게 갈아 건더기와 가라앉은 녹말을 함께 넣고 반죽하여 기름에 지진 음식이다. 많은 재료가 필요 없고 만드는 방법도 간단하여 쉽게 만들어 먹을 수 있다. 고소하고 쫀득한 감자전은 김치전, 빈대떡과 함께 비 오는 날 생각나게 하는 간식 겸 반찬이다. 개운하고 칼칼한 맛을 위해 풋고추, 양파 등을 같이 넣어 만들기도 한다.

Let's Speak Korean! p.171

감자를 사러 가요.
'V+-(으)러 가다'는 어떤 곳에 가는 이유나 목적을 나타낼 때 사용하는 표현이다.

감자가 얼마예요?
'얼마예요?'는 물건의 가격을 물을 때 쓰는 표현이다. '100g에'에서 '에'는 'for', 'per'의 의미이며, 가격을 읽을 때에는 한자어 숫자를 사용한다.

호박죽 Hobakjuk p.172

호박죽은 늙은 호박을 삶아 으깨어 찹쌀가루를 넣고 끓인 죽이다. 호박죽의 황금빛의 고운 색깔과 부드럽고 달콤한 맛이 눈과 입을 즐겁게 한다. 예전에는 집집마다 호박을 키워 열매와 잎, 순을 다양하게 조리하여 모두 먹었다. 호박죽은 부드럽고 부담이 없어서 아침 식사로 또는 식전 음식이나 간식으로 먹는다. 호박죽은 칼로리가 낮아 다이어트 음식으로도 활용된다.

Let's Speak Korean! p.175

삶기 전에 불리세요.
'V+-기 전에'는 어떤 행동이나 상태가 다른 행동이나 상태보다 앞서는 것을 나타낼 때 사용하는 표현이다.

호박부터 잘라 주세요.
'부터'는 어떤 일이나 상태 따위에 관련된 범위의 시작임을 나타내는 조사이며, 명사 뒤에 붙여 쓴다. 끝을 나타내는 '까지'가 뒤에 오는 경우가 많다.

핫도그 Hot dog p.176

핫도그는 나무 꼬치에 소시지나 치즈를 끼우고 밀가루 반죽으로 감싸서 튀긴 뒤 설탕과 케첩, 머스터드 등을 뿌려 먹는 간식의 한 종류이다. 예전에는 소시지가 들어 있는 핫도그만 있었지만 최근에는 소시지 대신 모차렐라 치즈를 넣은 치즈 핫도그가 인기가 많다. 핫도그는 서양의 hot dog가 한국에 들어와 변주된 것으로 마치 hot dog에 막대를 꽂은 것처럼 보이지만 만드는 방법과 맛이 많이 다르다.

Let's Speak Korean! p.179

소시지나 치즈 있어요?
'N+(이)나'는 둘 이상의 사물을 같은 자격으로 연결하면서 그 사물 중 하나만이 선택됨을 나타낼 때 사용한다.

요리를 잘해요?
'을/를 잘하다(동사)'는 '을/를'의 대상이 되는 것을 능숙하게 수행할 수 있다는 의미를 나타내는 표현이다. 이에 반대 되는 표현은 '을/를 못하다(동사)'이다.

짜파구리 Jjapaguri p.180

영화 '기생충'에 등장했던 '짜파구리'는 영화가 세계적으로 흥행을 하면서 함께 유명해진 한국 음식이다. '짜파구리'는 '짜파게티'라는 라면의 앞 2글자와 '너구리'라는 라면의 뒤 2글자를 합쳐서 붙여진 이름이다. 짜파구리는 이름처럼 조리법과 맛이 전혀 다른 두 가지 라면을 함께 조리하여 그 맛이 매우 독특하다. 더군다나 여기에 영화에서처럼 소고기 채끝살을 함께 먹으면 맛과 영양이 풍부해진다.

Let's Speak Korean! p.183

3분 더 끓이세요.
'3분'의 '분'은 시간을 읽는 단위이다. '분'을 읽을 때에는 고유어 숫자를 사용한다.

열한 시예요.
'11시'의 '시'는 시간을 읽는 단위 중 '시간'을 의미한다. '시'의 숫자 부분을 읽을 때에는 한자어 숫자를 사용한다.

Index of Ingredients

Index of Cooking Vocabulary